P.S. Please Write Back

Snail mail correspondence encouragement and ideas.

Large Print 18 point

Paula Nafziger

Title.................................P.S. Please Write Back
Subtitle ....Snail mail correspondence encouragement and ideas.
.................................Large Print 18 point type
Type ....Trade Paperback (US), Large Print
Author ....Paula Nafziger
Subject Heading.....................Family & Relationships, Parenting
ISBN-13 ....9781639420056 .... 9 8 7 6 5 4 3 2 1

©2021 Paula Nafziger, All rights reserved
Publisher: NAFCO-Inc., PO Box 5529, Diamond Bar, CA 91765

Printed in the U.S.A. 082321

P.S. Please Write Back

Table of Contents

Make Mail Interesting 5
The Four D's 7
The Benefits of writing GREAT letters 9
Conversation Starters 13
Apology Wording Ideas 71
Fishing for a Response 87
Nicely Worded Statements 95
Positive Words List 107
Questions You Might Ask 121
Statements/Questions to Talk with Teens ... 125
Things Kids Might Want to Know 127
Loving Letter Endings 129
Abbreviations & Acronyms 131
Emoticons & Doodle Art 135
Line Guide 137

Make Mail Interesting

When I was a child, my grandma often sent handwritten cards and letters by mail. Unlike bills and junk mail to my parents, it was a big thrill to find something in the mailbox addressed to me! Grandma ended her letters with a relationship-building request:

P.S. Please write back.

Life today seems markedly complicated for children, their parents, relatives, and loved ones. Many adults have to navigate a relationship with their children while dealing with caregivers, court custody orders, work-related travel requirements, government or municipal agencies, hospital or prison visiting rules, military deployment, and so on. Challenges like these limit the ability to communicate and bond with a child while apart, or know, understand, and relate to them when present.

Separations, whether for short or long durations, can be life-changing for both adults and children. While some parents can communicate using modern technology, others are prevented from any form of virtual contact. Good old-fashioned postal service may be the only means of connecting and communicating. Letters from a loving but absent parent are usually cherished indefinitely and read repeatedly. Words are powerful, and written words are even more so.

Some parents are prohibited from sending correspondence to their children until they reach adulthood. In this case, the adult is encouraged to write from their heart now then save cards and letters to give to the child later in life.

I hope this book encourages you to gain empathy from a child's perspective and communicate with them as much as possible. It will take effort to foster a loving relationship by mail.

Ideally, you will think beyond what is included within this book and be inspired to create new ways to make your mail interesting, inviting, read, **and responded to!**

The Four D's

When you communicate by handwritten letters, it is usually best to start with simple things. Begin with basic subjects and information you believe will be comfortable for both sides. As you become familiar with each other, your attitude, intent, and tone are less likely to be misinterpreted. Trust begins to develop. Over time you'll be able to reveal stronger emotions, feelings, opinions, and viewpoints with less chance of offending each other. *The best way to establish a relationship is to be more interested in the other person's interests and values than your own.* The type of communication you share will likely be in the style of debate, dialogue, diatribe, or discourse:

Debates tend to be competitive to "win" an argument. Having a debate with someone can effectively convince someone of facts and truths. Still, it tends to alienate and hinder rather than unite and encourage additional communication.

Dialogue is the most common way to have a conversation with your loved one, usually in person, by communicating back and forth. Writing "dialogue style" means you write as though the person was with you, asking questions, sharing intimately, then waiting for answers. This is the best way to develop a relationship because it builds on mutual respect, input, and feedback.

Diatribe is one-sided to express your emotions and feelings while criticizing those who disagree with you. Although a diatribe effectively lets others know your opinions, an angry rant or scolding can alienate and cause distance in a relationship, *so use it cautiously*. On the positive side, a diatribe can inspire and unite those who share your same perspective.

Discourse involves communicating logic, premises, rationale, reasoning, and various thoughts as though you were giving a lecture. Its purpose is to deliver information. When used lovingly, it has its place as a way to convey information and teach.

The Benefits of writing GREAT letters to Kids

- Adults and children can encourage each other.
- Children need encouragement as they try to overcome difficulties.
- Children often feel more connected to their absent loved ones.
- It helps encourage, develop, or reinforce a relationship.
- It offers a way to bond by sharing experiences with each other.
- Letter writing improves communication skills.
- Letters are often kept indefinitely (and read over and over again).
- Letters can motivate others to make better choices.
- Mail is something adults and children usually look forward to.
- Parental advice can be shared despite being apart from their child.
- Writers and readers improve in language, spelling, handwriting, etc.
- Writers and receivers experience joy, love, and a sense of belonging.

G **Greet**

R **Recall** When possible, refer back to your child's last letter to you. Ask for more information on anything your child shared in their previous communication. This will show an interest in what they are going through or what they find important. Answer any questions they asked.

E **Express** Convey your thoughts, feelings, hopes, dreams, etc., with your child. Write about what you find important, valuable, etc. Remember to think about your child's age and what <u>they</u> would find interesting from your life experiences.

A **Ask** Ask your child questions that you would like to know answers to and questions that might prompt them to write back.

T **Ta ta for now** End your letter with something memorable as a cute way to send your love. Some people use TTFN (ta ta for now, popular in WWII) meaning goodbye but let's talk/visit again soon. Others are: PWB (please write back), SWAK (sealed or sent with a kiss), XOXO (X=Hugs O=Kisses), PS (postscript).

Alpacas spit if annoyed or angry. If you see their tail switch back and forth, watch out!

Conversation Starters

Use the following questions to encourage verbal or written communication with your loved one:

1. A "chance encounter" that changed my life was:
2. An activity I've never tried but want to is:
3. A fond memory from my neighborhood is:
4. A question I've love to get an answer to or response about is:
5. Addiction has affected me in "this" manner:
6. After this person died, I didn't grieve well and made these bad decisions:
7. Alcohol has affected my life in "this" way:
8. Although it would be nice to be perfect, I know I'm not because:
9. Although others are obsessed with "this," I am not:
10. Although the courts might separate us, we will always be family, and I will always:
11. An amazing adventure I'd love to have is:
12. Are you religious or spiritual, and if so, what or whom would you most identify with—and what are your beliefs?
13. As a child, I used to feel a sense of guilt for "this," but I now realize it was FALSE guilt—it wasn't my fault, so I'd like to communicate about it with you to help me get through this struggle for truth:
14. As your parent, this is how I see our future:
15. At age ___, my "teen idol" was:
16. At least once in my life, I hope to:
17. At least once in my life, I wish I could:
18. At least once in your life, you should:
19. At this time, I am concentrating on:
20. Because I love you, I worry about:
21. Because I still have breath, I still have time to correct mistakes so, I am choosing to:
22. Because I wasn't in my right mind, can you

Role reversal: Male bat-eared foxes are the parental caregivers. Their ears are 5" tall.

Conversation Starters

share how my behavior affected you?

23. Because I wasn't in my right mind, can you share what happened when:
24. Because I wasn't in my right mind, can you share what you know about:
25. Because of where I am, it might not be healthy but I've trained myself not to cry about this:
26. Can you help me understand why you struggle with:
27. Can you share an example of when you had to make the best of a bad situation:
28. Can you share some gifts, skills, or talents you believe I possess which I could develop further?
29. Can you share something you are interested in, that I don't pay attention to you about?
30. Can you share something you think I don't listen to you about?
31. Can you share why you don't want to talk about:
32. Can you think of anything good, helpful, or positive I've ever told you that you repeat to others?
33. Can you think of anything I've ever said that harmed you?
34. Can you think of anything I've ever said that helped you?
35. Communicating with you is hard because:
36. Conflict makes me:
37. Constructive criticism helps a person learn. List at least one thing I need to understand:
38. Could you find it in your heart to forgive me for:
39. Describe a family tradition you still keep:
40. Describe a funny story about a pet:
41. Describe a funny story about a sibling:
42. Describe a time when you laughed to the point of crying:
43. Describe one "stupid kid" moment you've had:
44. Describe the last time you thought, "what am I doing?":

P.S. Please Write Back

Conversation Starters

45 Describe your "best moment" this year, month, or week:
46 Describe your happiest birthday memory:
47 Describe your idea of a "family fun night":
48 Do you get along with those you live with right now?
49 Do you keep a journal, or do you write out your thoughts?
50 Do you remember a time when I lost my patience, so we can talk it through, and I can apologize?
51 Do you remember the time I:
52 Do you remember the time you:
53 Do you remember this?
54 Do you remember when:
55 Do you think it is futile to hope "this"?
56 Doing "this" usually causes me to fall asleep:
57 Drugs have affected my life in this way:
58 Drugs have affected your life in this way:
59 Even if the courts force the "termination of my parental rights" don't ever forget this:
60 Even though I have made mistakes, it doesn't change _____.
61 Even though people generally discount what I say, "this" is really true:
62 Even though we are far by distance, I feel emotionally close, bonded to you when:
63 Even though we'll be apart on your birthday, you and I can both do this from a distance:
64 Ever since I saw "this," I've struggled with that image:
65 Every Christmas without you, I feel this way:
66 Every year on your birthday I do "this":
67 Every year on your birthday I feel this way:
68 Everyone I know doubted I could do "this":
69 Everything got so messed up when:
70 Everything I have done has affected more than myself. How has it affected you?

Bee-eater birds have bright-colored feathers and eat bees, wasps, and other insects.

Conversation Starters

71 Finances are difficult at my house because:
72 Finish the sentence with something clean and interesting: When I was your age I...
73 Finish the sentence: It really annoys me when...
74 Finish this sentence: I hate. . .
75 For as long as I can remember I:
76 From my perspective and experience around others, alcohol does this:
77 From my perspective and experience around others, drugs do this:
78 From my perspective and experience around others, illegal behavior does this:
79 Having someone else decide that we can't be with each other is hard because:
80 Healing our relationship is painful because:
81 Here are some specific steps that might help you in the challenge you shared with me:
82 Here are three things I would like to accomplish this year/month/week:
83 Here is how you could help me let go of:
84 Here is one dream I have for you:
85 Here is one good memory I have of us:
86 Here is one hope I have for you:
87 Here is something I admire about you:
88 Here is something I didn't value at the time and now regret it:
89 Here is something I respect you about:
90 Here is the story of how you got the nickname I call you:
91 Here is what I think would happen if I spent a lot of time with you in the future:
92 How are you feeling right now?
93 How can I be the most helpful to you at this time in your life?
94 How did you feel when you learned we would be apart?

P.S. Please Write Back

Conversation Starters

95	How does my medical condition affect you?
96	How has our family helped you?
97	How has our family unit harmed you?
98	How have your relationships with friends changed since we have been apart?
99	How much time do you spend in your place, house, room, etc.?
100	How would you describe life with dad?
101	How would you describe life with mom?
102	How would you describe your childhood:
103	How would you respond to this statement: "Getting arrested was good because..."?
104	I accept individual responsibility for:
105	I accept responsibility for "this" and apologize to you because:
106	I accidentally forgot to do this important thing:
107	I admire you for this:
108	I always get/got in trouble for "this" in school:
109	I always think of you when:
110	I am determined to:
111	I am determined to:
112	I am doing this to get ready to reunite with you someday:
113	I am happy today because:
114	I am having a hard time over:
115	I am hurting because:
116	I am learning to ignore:
117	I am learning to:
118	I am most blessed/proud of "this" creation/invention of mine:
119	I am not as rough as I sound because:
120	I am not as tough as I appear because:
121	I am not good at expressing my feelings because:
122	I am not looking forward to:
123	I am really sorry I made you feel:

Bison (Buffalo) can grow to 11 feet high, 2200 pounds, and still, run up to 40 mph.

Conversation Starters

124. I am really sorry about my actions/behavior/words. Can you share one thing we could talk about?
125. I am sorry that the last time we were together I:
126. I am still mad about:
127. I am striving toward self-improvement by doing this:
128. I am struggling with "this":
129. I am tired of hearing about:
130. I am trying to face the impact my choices have made on you in this:
131. I am trying to forgive you for:
132. I am trying to gain more control over "this" about me:
133. I am very upset by what I did when:
134. I am very upset by what I said when:
135. I apologize for disrespecting you when:
136. I appreciate that you are strong enough to admit this:
137. I become sad that you:
138. I believe I will never experience:
139. I believe in and/or support "this" charity, religious organization, or cause because:
140. I believe you help my self-esteem because:
141. I blame myself for:
142. I can enjoy watching this movie/tv show over-and-over again:
143. I can express myself best here:
144. I can only hope that you forgive me even though I:
145. I can talk about almost anything with "this" person:
146. I can't describe how painful this is:
147. I can't even explain how wonderful it feels when:
148. I can't get this image/scene out of my memory:
149. I can't make the guilt I feel go away over:
150. I can't talk to you about "this" right now, but hope to in the future:
151. I can't seem to get this image out of my mind:

P.S. Please Write Back

Conversation Starters

152 I can't talk to you about "this":
153 I care about you so much because:
154 I constantly worry about:
155 I cried out for help when this happened:
156 I cry almost every day because:
157 I cry when:
158 I didn't think I would like "this" until I tried it:
159 I didn't use to believe my dad about "this":
160 I didn't use to believe my mom about "this":
161 I don't always do the right thing, in the right way, or at the right time because:
162 I don't always say the right thing, in the right way, or at the right time because:
163 I don't feel comfortable in the presence of:
164 I don't feel you understand this:
165 I don't get to talk to you often enough about this:
166 I don't intentionally mean to hurt you, and:
167 I don't know if the hurt of "this" will ever go away:
168 I don't know what to do when this happens:
169 I don't like that you:
170 I don't like to watch "this":
171 I don't live with this person, but he/she helps me:
172 I don't often cry around others because:
173 I don't tell my friends the truth about you because:
174 I don't tell my friends where you are because:
175 I don't think it is fair that:
176 I don't think you realize this:
177 I don't understand this:
178 I don't understand why you:
179 I don't want to be like you in this:
180 I don't want to show the way I feel because:
181 I don't want to visit you at this time because:

Wild boar groups are called "sounds." The upper lip tusk on males sharpens the lower tusks.

Conversation Starters

182 I don't write you often because:
183 I dream about:
184 I enjoy watching:
185 I experienced "this" amazing thing, but no one was there to witness it with me:
186 I feel a heavy burden of guilt because:
187 I feel awkward when:
188 I feel bonded to you because:
189 I feel closer to you because:
190 I feel convicted about my role as:
191 I feel desperate when:
192 I feel empowered when:
193 I feel happy when:
194 I feel I am maturing in this area:
195 I feel I can learn from my mistakes because:
196 I feel judged about "this":
197 I feel responsible for:
198 I feel so restricted by:
199 I feel sports help:
200 I feel stripped of my dignity when:
201 I feel uncomfortable when:
202 I feel unstoppable when:
203 I feel very close to you because:
204 I feel very motivated to change in this way:
205 I felt so cared for by you when:
206 I felt so loved by you when:
207 I felt unappreciated when:
208 I find it interesting when you write about:
209 I get emotional when:
210 I get excited when:
211 I get fired up and full of passion when:
212 I get in trouble because:

Conversation Starters

213 I get nervous when:
214 I get scared sometimes because:
215 I get too competitive when:
216 I get too passionate about "this":
217 I get too upset about:
218 I get very anxious because:
219 I had a good dream about:
220 I had a terrible nightmare about:
221 I hate feeling obligated to:
222 I hate holding in my emotions but:
223 I have "this" fond memory of you and me together:
224 I have a hard time confronting my past on this:
225 I have a hard time forgiving you about:
226 I have a hard time forgiving you because:
227 I have a hard time forgiving:
228 I have a hard time letting you in my life because:
229 I have a hard time telling you:
230 I have a hard time trusting you because:
231 I have a strong opinion about:
232 I have always been close to you because:
233 I have been self-focused about:
234 I have conflicted feelings about:
235 I have kept all your cards, letters, and art, but this is one of my favorites:
236 I have let go of most of my anger about:
237 I have lost or gained weight because:
238 I have missed out on "this" because:
239 I have never felt so much shame as when:
240 I have problems, and this is one I'd like to communicate with you about:
241 I have promised myself that:
242 I have something important to share, which is:

Brown bear "Grizzlies" weigh up to 1700 pounds yet climb trees and run up to 35 mph.

Conversation Starters

243 I have so much I want to communicate with you about, so here is one thing:
244 I hope I never experience "this":
245 I hope to spend eternity with you and:
246 I hurt when:
247 I isn't easy when:
248 I keep meaning to do "this," but haven't yet
249 I kind of "lose my mind" when I experience, hear, or see "this":
250 I know every communication won't always be easy, or positive, but I promise to:
251 I know everyone messes up and makes mistakes, so I'm going to:
252 I know from the bottom of my heart that:
253 I know how to play these/this musical instrument(s):
254 I know I wasn't there for you when:
255 I know I've "put you through hell" by my poor decision-making. What could we write about that would help you begin healing?
256 I know I've burned bridges, but I ask forgiveness for:
257 I know I've put you through a lot of pain and tears. What can I do now to help you begin or continue healing?
258 I know it's impossible to forget, but do you think you could ever forgive me for:
259 I know it's not "the end of the world," but this is still hard:
260 I know the decisions I make this year, month, or week will affect my future in this way:
261 I know you don't have super-powers like a cartoon, so I am choosing to accept this:
262 I know you say you love me, but this confuses me:
263 I laugh when:
264 I laughed to the point of crying when:

P.S. Please Write Back

Conversation Starters

265	I learned this bad habit. What advice can you offer to help me change?
266	I learned to respect you more because:
267	I like it when you:
268	I like to do "this" the old fashioned way:
269	I like to keep in touch with you because:
270	I like to make art/creative writing for you because:
271	I like to receive art/creative writing from you because:
272	I like to share my little secrets with you because:
273	I like to share new ideas with you about:
274	I like to talk with you about:
275	I like to watch people do "this":
276	I like to write about:
277	I look forward to you being a big part of my life when:
278	I look up to my dad because:
279	I look up to my mom because:
280	I love it when you just listen to me because:
281	I love it when you:
282	I love to listen to "this" person the most:
283	I love/loved doing "this" with my brother:
284	I love/loved doing "this" with my Dad:
285	I love/loved doing "this" with my family:
286	I love/loved doing "this" with my grandparent(s):
287	I love/loved doing "this" with my Mom:
288	I love/loved doing "this" with my sister:
289	I made "this" mistake, but it's my fault alone:
290	I made a mistake and now:
291	I make the best:
292	I messed up, and now it affects you. What are you going through because of my wrong decision(s)?
293	I miss that we used to:
294	I miss you so much it feels like:

Wild burros are a danger to drivers along Lake Havasu and Parker, Arizona roadways.

Conversation Starters

295 I miss you this much:
296 I need advice about:
297 I need encouragement from you in this way:
298 I need encouragement in this area:
299 I need more guidance or wisdom about:
300 I need resources to get help regarding:
301 I need space to grow about:
302 I need to develop myself in:
303 I need to give more of "this" away:
304 I need to hear positive statements/thoughts on this:
305 I need to learn to resist "this":
306 I need to put "this" behind me:
307 I need to seek someone out to show me:
308 I need your support in this way:
309 I never realized how blind I was to:
310 I never realized that:
311 I never want to do this again:
312 I now realize how stupid and blind I was when:
313 I once laughed inappropriately because:
314 I once turned red-faced blush when "this" happened:
315 I owe an apology to:
316 I pray about this a lot:
317 I proved my critics wrong when:
318 I really enjoy "this" simple little thing:
319 I received difficult news this year/month/week, which was:
320 I regret not doing "this" when I was young:
321 I regret:
322 I rejected "this" but shouldn't have:
323 I remember when you used to:
324 I respect you for this:
325 I sacrificed "this" to get "this":
326 I see you as:

Conversation Starters

327 I shouldn't have:
328 I sometimes have nightmares, and "this" was the worst:
329 I sometimes need:
330 I spend the most time thinking about:
331 I still have an emotional/physical scar from:
332 I still have fond memories of "this" gift from you:
333 I still have fond memories of giving you "this":
334 I still regret throwing this away:
335 I struggle with "this":
336 I struggle with anger over:
337 I struggle with not maintaining self-control. I apologize for:
338 I struggle with school mostly because:
339 I struggle with the hurt of knowing:
340 I survived "this" harrowing situation:
341 I tell you about the mistakes I have made because:
342 I think "this" could help our family remain close even though we are apart:
343 I think "this" is a really bad idea:
344 I think "this" would help us form a healthier relationship:
345 I think "this" would help us have a positive relationship:
346 I think "this" would help us move forward in our relationship:
347 I think about what we used to do, and this is one of my favorite memories:
348 I think everyone should obey "this" rule:
349 I think it is important to stay in touch because:
350 I think it is more important to be loyal to my (pick one: family, friends, gang) because:
351 I think of you every day, and every night. Here are some of my thoughts:
352 I think our relationship is getting better because:
353 I think support in this area would really benefit me:
354 I thought I was outsmarting everyone when I:

Arabian camels weigh up to 1400 pounds. They huff, spit, kick and bite when annoyed.

Conversation Starters

355   I took a giant "leap of faith" when I:
356   I try to understand your situation but can't because:
357   I use this to help me learn what is right and wrong:
358   I used to be "this":
359   I used to covet "this," but I'm glad I never got it:
360   I used to do "this":
361   I used to have "a crush (intense infatuation) for/on:
362   I used to play or hang out with this person, but now I don't because:
363   I used to think you were "perfect," but now I understand no one is because:
364   I want to apologize for being:
365   I want to apologize for doing:
366   I want to apologize for saying:
367   I want to apologize for:
368   I want to be a real (but flawed) person rather than fake. What do you know about me that I need to address or discuss?
369   I want to be closer in our relationship and feel "this" needs to happen:
370   I want to be like you in this:
371   I want to let go of:
372   I want to live in honesty, which means I need to confess:
373   I want to make my future better because:
374   I want to share about a decision I need to make:
375   I want to talk about the time I made this promise but didn't keep it:
376   I want to talk about the time you made this promise but didn't keep it:
377   I want to tell you everything I can about:
378   I want to thank you for accepting me when:
379   I want to thank you for being loving when:

P.S. Please Write Back

Conversation Starters

380 I want to thank you for caring about me when:
381 I want to thank you for helping me when:
382 I want to thank you for listening to me when:
383 I want to thank you for teaching me:
384 I want to thank you for:
385 I want to trust you but:
386 I want you to know I miss being in your life daily and:
387 I was "there" when:
388 I was blinded by greed and pride when:
389 I was disrespectful when:
390 I was given my name or nickname because:
391 I was really disappointed when this happened:
392 I was really scared when this happened:
393 I was really touched when I saw:
394 I was severely affected when this person died:
395 I was so dumb I thought I'd never be caught (but I was) for:
396 I was such a fool not to:
397 I was the one who was wrong in this situation:
398 I was too selfish to realize my poor decision would cause you:
399 I was unkind when:
400 I was used to help save a persons life in "this" way:
401 I was wrong when:
402 I wasn't thinking straight when:
403 I wasn't there for "this," and regret it:
404 I wish I "wasn't in the dark" about this:
405 I wish I could ask my dad "this":
406 I wish I could ask my mom "this":
407 I wish I could be honest with others about you but:
408 I wish I could be honest with you about:
409 I wish I could meet:
410 I wish I could watch "this" scene of my life:
411 I wish I had a better relationship with:

✗ Capybara hop similar to rabbits, bark like dogs, and are big, measuring 53"w x 24"h.

Conversation Starters

412   I wish I had paid better attention in "this" class:
413   I wish I hadn't ever seen this:
414   I wish I knew how to make:
415   I wish I were better at:
416   I wish I was more responsible at:
417   I wish I would stop:
418   I wish my brain was better at:
419   I wish people would listen to my dad when he says:
420   I wish people would listen to my mom when she says:
421   I wish they still had "this":
422   I wish we could talk more about:
423   I wish you hadn't:
424   I wish you would communicate more about:
425   I wish you would share more about "this":
426   I wish you would tell me more stories of your life because:
427   I wished I had listened to _____ about:
428   I won't ever forget "this" day because:
429   I won't ever forget "this":
430   I worry you are hanging out with the "wrong crowd" because:
431   I would appreciate it if you could pray about:
432   I would like to be involved in the decision to:
433   I would like to know "this" about you:
434   I would like to work on improving:
435   I would like you to re-enter my life, but I know it might be hard because:
436   I wouldn't want my worst enemy to experience:
437   I write you long letters because:
438   I write you often because:
439   I'm sad today because:
440   I'd be terrible at:
441   I'd like to be closer in our relationship and think "this" would help us:

Conversation Starters

442 I'd like to try "this" but haven't because:
443 I'd like to try:
444 I'd liked to be remembered for:
445 I'd love to be a part of "this" team/group because:
446 I'd love to be able to control:
447 I'd love to go to:
448 I'd love to have "this" job, at "this" company:
449 I'd love to solve this mystery:
450 I'm afraid to tell others about:
451 I'm afraid you could love me less if I:
452 I'm afraid you will reject me if I tell you:
453 I'm afraid you won't love me if I tell you:
454 I'm curious about:
455 I'm glad I got through "this" disease/injury/surgery:
456 I'm glad that I will never lose you, no matter what others say or do because:
457 I'm most famous for:
458 I'm not afraid to tell others about:
459 I'm not always sure why, but sometimes I:
460 I'm not kidding, one day "this" happened:
461 I'm not sure you know that when you do "this", I don't feel good about it:
462 I'm not very good at communicating what I really think and feel because:
463 I'm not too proud to ask for help in this:
464 I'm pretty religious about:
465 I'm pretty terrible at:
466 I'm proud of you because:
467 I'm proud of you when:
468 I'm really struggling today. Could you keep me in your prayers/thoughts about:
469 I'm still a little mad about:

Cats can sleep up to 12 hours a day, have retractable claws, and hate citrus smells.

Conversation Starters

470 I'm still amazed I won "this":
471 I'm trying to change for the better in this area:
472 I'm trying to follow in your footsteps by:
473 I'm trying to learn to be:
474 I've been in a talent contest for:
475 I've learned "this" from you:
476 If a "genie in a bottle" were real, what three things would you wish for?
477 If education, experience, location, money, or opportunity wasnot a problem; I would do this:
478 If Fall is a time of letting go, Winter is a time of reflection, Spring is a time of hope, and Summer is a time of freedom, what season are you in at this time, and why?
479 If I am bored, can you give one suggestion of something positive/productive I could do?
480 If I could ask God one question, it would be:
481 If I could ask you one thing, it would be:
482 If I could forget one thing, it would be:
483 If I could get you to forget "this," it would be:
484 If I could have observed or been present for "this," I:
485 If I could master one skill, it would be:
486 If I could only share one problem I've had in the last month or week, I'd say it was:
487 If I could persuade you to do something, it would be to:
488 If I could press a restart button, this is how I would parent differently:
489 If I could travel anywhere in the world, I'd pick:
490 If I could visit with you right now, I'd share:
491 If I don't write often, it's not because I don't love you. It's because:
492 If I had to sing a song in front of a loved one, I'd choose:
493 If I had unlimited money and time, I would:

Conversation Starters

494 If I knew I couldn't fail, I would:
495 If I said, "things are going to be different," what would that look like to you?
496 If I started my own business, it would be:
497 If lessons were free, I'd like to learn:
498 If money were not an issue, what hobby would you enjoy?
499 If somehow this letter never gets delivered to you I hope someday:
500 If someone handed you a $20 bill, how would you use it?
501 If someone harms me, I promise to tell you right away:
502 If someone in the family is ill, please don't keep it from me because:
503 If someone makes a mistake, there is a consequence at some point. Mine is:
504 If something happened to you or me this year, what do you think either of us might regret not discussing?
505 If something happened to you or me this year, what do you think either of us might regret not saying?
506 If something happened to you or me this year, what do you think either of us might regret?
507 If the courts force a "termination of my parental rights" just know I will still:
508 If there is only one subject I am upset about often, it is:
509 If we could have a friendly debate about "this" I would choose the topic of:
510 If we switched places for a day, what advice would you give me?
511 If we were together right now, this is what I think would be fun to do:
512 If you are free to come back into my life regularly, I hope:
513 If you asked me to explore my feelings about "this" it would be:

Cattle: Scottish Highlander (hairy cows) outer coat measures up to 13" long.

Conversation Starters

514 If you can make the best of a bad situation, so can I, so I'm going to:
515 If you can't control "this," at least you can control "this":
516 If you can't sleep, what is the usual cause or reason?
517 If you could ask God one question, what would it be?
518 If you could choose any acre of land, where would you choose it to be?
519 If you knew I would take it, what advice would you offer?
520 If you could live in a big city, which one would you choose?
521 If you could live in a small town, which one would you choose?
522 If you could observe or be present for one event, what would it be?
523 If you could only have one electronic item what would you choose and why?
524 If you could only share one main issue you are facing now, you would say:
525 If you could start your own business, what would it be?
526 If you could take any class in the world, what would you choose to educate yourself on?
527 If you could win a contest, what would it be for?
528 If you could, what skill would you like to master?
529 If you feel I don't understand how guilty I should feel about something, what would you say it is?
530 If you had a million bucks, how would you help others?
531 If you had to describe my personality to a friend, what would you most likely say?
532 If you had to eat one plate of food every day for a week, what would you put on that plate?
533 If you had to name your "teen idol," who would you say it is/was?

Conversation Starters

534 If you had unlimited money and time, what would you choose to do with it?
535 If you have a hard time listening to me talk about something, what is it?
536 If you have ever been in a commercial, movie, the news, or TV, what was that experience like?
537 If you have you ever felt I've forgotten you, what made you feel that way?
538 If you know now what you did was wrong, why did the mistake seem reasonable at the time?
539 If you share with me everything I've done that has affected you negatively, I promise to address each issue. What is one of the things I need to communicate with you about?
540 If you still have an emotional/physical scar from something, share more:
541 If you told me everything, in what ways do you feel it would change the way I feel about you?
542 If you were here with me right now, this is what I'd want you to know:
543 If you were in my shoes, how would you solve "this" dilemma?
544 If you were more responsible, it would help in "this":
545 If you were recognized as "an expert" at something, what would it most likely be?
546 If you would communicate about "this," it might help me get through:
547 If you would communicate more about this, it would help me:
548 If you wouldn't get mad or angry, I wish we could talk about:
549 If you've ever been used to help save a person's life, what happened?
550 Illegal behavior has affected my life in this way:
551 Illegal behavior has affected your life in this way:

Cheetahs are the fastest animal in the world, reaching 70 mph in three seconds!

Conversation Starters

552 In my eyes, "this" person is a hero because:
553 In my free time, I often:
554 To visit with you in person, I have to:
555 In what ways do we think alike?
556 In what ways do we think differently?
557 In what ways do you feel alcohol has affected your life?
558 In what ways do you feel drugs have affected your life?
559 In what ways do you think how you were raised influences who you are today?
560 In what ways do you think illegal behavior has affected your life?
561 In what ways is it possible to love someone who isn't perfect?
562 In your opinion, what is the most exciting sport to watch, play, or hear?
563 Is there anything I've ever said or called you, that still rings in your ear today?
564 Is there something you think I don't "get" about you?
565 It felt good when you used to:
566 It hurts when:
567 It is boring or dreadful to attend "this":
568 It makes me happy that you are open to talk about:
569 It upset me when you made an excuse about:
570 It was hard when "this" person saw:
571 It was hard when I was younger because:
572 It's hard to build a relationship because:
573 It's hard to communicate because:
574 It's impossible not to cry when:
575 Just by looking at me, you'd never know I:
576 Kids need their parent(s) because:
577 Knowing I can't reverse my stupidity, what can I do now to help you moving forward?
578 Knowing you want me makes me feel:

Conversation Starters

579 Like all families, we have challenges. What is our biggest challenge from your point of view?
580 Looking back, I didn't care what I did or who I hurt when I:
581 Most people don't believe "this":
582 Most people who know me would be surprised to learn I:
583 My all-time favorite game to play is:
584 My attitude needs adjusting about:
585 My behavior was terrible when:
586 My conscience makes me want to:
587 My failure to do this helped me change, by choosing to do this:
588 My family has "this" special or unusual tradition:
589 My family is more important than my friends because:
590 My family seems dysfunctional because:
591 My family suffers because:
592 My favorite activity/hobby/pastime is:
593 My favorite book/movie/song/theater production/TV show is:
594 My favorite childhood memory is:
595 My favorite home-cooked meal is:
596 My favorite quote/line of poetry/sentence/verse is:
597 My favorite restaurant and meal is:
598 My favorite thing to do is?
599 My favorite thing to do when helping others is:
600 My greatest failure is "this," but it taught me:
601 My ideas differ from yours in these ways:
602 My judgment became cloudy when:
603 My least favorite home-cooked meal is:
604 My life is complicated because:
605 My life is hard because:
606 My life would be different if you were able to be with me now because:
607 My most embarrassing moment was:

Deer: doe or hind (female), buck or stag (male), chew food, regurgitate, and chew it again.

Conversation Starters

608 My most irrational/unusual fear is:
609 My outward smile isn't really how I feel on the inside because:
610 My parents encouraged me to:
611 My thoughts about alcohol are:
612 My thoughts about illegal drugs are:
613 My thoughts if I could observe or be present for "this" event:
614 My worst "customer service" experience was:
615 My worst "seemed like a good idea" moment was:
616 My worst animal experience was:
617 My worst cooking mishap was:
618 My worst epic fail was:
619 My worst ever getaway/vacation story is when:
620 My worst road-trip experience was:
621 Name a "turning point" in your life:
622 Name a date on the calendar that makes you feel happy:
623 Name a date on the calendar that makes you feel sad:
624 Name a time when you proved your critics wrong:
625 Name an experience where you felt unappreciated:
626 Name an incident when you felt uncomfortable because I didn't have a filter on my mouth:
627 Name one interest you have that you don't think I know yet:
628 Name one interest you have that you know I know:
629 Name one mystery you've love to solve:
630 Name one of your "defining moments" so far:
631 Name one simple little thing you really enjoy:
632 Name one thing you can't afford/obtain, but would love to have:
633 Name one thing you don't think I listen to you about:
634 Name one thing you don't think we can talk about, but should:
635 Name one thing you don't want to do:
636 Name one thing you feel I have done wrong:

P.S. Please Write Back

Conversation Starters

637 Name one thing you got for Christmas last year:
638 Name one thing you got for your Birthday:
639 Name one thing you need to give away more:
640 Name one thing you regret throwing away:
641 Name one thing you think I have done right:
642 Name one thing you wish you were able to make a decision about:
643 Name one thing you would like to see me do:
644 Name one thing you'd like to do someday:
645 Name someone you wish you had a better relationship with:
646 Name something that happens more often than you'd like:
647 Name something there is still time not to regret:
648 Name something you are pretty terrible at:
649 Name something you dislike but have to do:
650 Name something you feel you would be terrible at:
651 Name something you think would be boring or dreadful to attend:
652 Name something you will NEVER do again, and why:
653 Name something you wish your brain were better at:
654 Name something you'd say, "I make the best":
655 Name something you've rejected, but later realized you shouldn't have:
656 Name the fanciest place you've ever been to:
657 Name three things you would like to accomplish this year/month/week:
658 Name two or three things you can think of that would help you heal?
659 Not being with you makes me:
660 Not many people know I'm good at:
661 Of past mistakes, I wish we could communicate about:
662 On your birthday this year there is a lot we can't do, but this is something we could do:

Chinese Crested dogs are "cat-like." They enjoy sitting in high places and catching rats.

Conversation Starters

663 Often, "this" makes my day better:
664 One "pet name" or nickname I love to remember you by is "this" because:
665 One "stupid kid" moment in my life was:
666 One day, I hope to realize "this" dream:
667 One day, I hope to:
668 One family tradition I've kept up is:
669 One goal I have accomplished this year/month/week is:
670 One memorable "family history" story I know is:
671 One memory I wish I could get rid of is:
672 One of the best things my parents ever did for me is:
673 One of the many dumb things I've learned is:
674 One of the most important moments for me was/is/will be:
675 One of the stupidest things I've ever done is:
676 One thing I can't afford/obtain but would love to have is:
677 One thing I dislike but have to do is:
678 One thing I've changed my belief/opinion about is:
679 One time I got mad at you about "this" and it still bugs me because:
680 One time when we talked, I wasn't right because:
681 One year/month/week ago, my life was very different because:
682 Pain from my past comes crashing down on me when:
683 Parenting is probably the most difficult job in the world. I hope to change at this:
684 People come to me for advice or help in "this":
685 People often misunderstand "this" about me:
686 People often misunderstand "this" about me:
687 People often misunderstand "this" about you:
688 People sometimes think I look like:
689 People think I remind them of:
690 Please share why you told me "this" when it wasn't true:

Conversation Starters

691 PSTD affects me in this way:
692 Reconnecting with you is hard because:
693 Regarding "this," am I doomed to follow in your footsteps?
694 School or work is hard because:
695 Share a good memory about your dad:
696 Share a good memory about your mom:
697 Share about a time when you felt awkward:
698 Share about a time when you got "red-faced blush" because "this" happened:
699 Share about a time you laughed inappropriately:
700 Share about a time you took a giant "leap of faith":
701 Share about the worst natural disaster you've ever experienced:
702 Share if you've ever been in a harrowing situation:
703 Share something you don't think I can handle:
704 Share something you wish you could for
705 Since I can't change other people, I would like to change this about myself:
706 Since my past is not my future, I am:
707 Since you are different from me, how does that affect you?
708 Some things you share "just don't add up". Can you clear this up?
709 Some days, I lose hope but I do this and realize tomorrow is another chance at a better future:
710 Something I can't/won't live without is:
711 Something I have/had taken for granted is/was:
712 Something I should do before the year ends is:
713 Something I think you are really good at is:
714 Something I will NEVER do again is:
715 Something I will never forget is:
716 Something I'd like but could never afford is:
717 Sometimes calls, email, mail, or visits are painful because:

Wood ducks are brightly colored. They use their claws to perch and nest in trees.

Conversation Starters

718 Sometimes I act as though I don't have problems because:
719 Sometimes I act dumb about:
720 Sometimes I act out physically because:
721 Sometimes I act out, and the reason why is:
722 Sometimes I am cold and distant because:
723 Sometimes I am disgusted by:
724 Sometimes I am frustrated because:
725 Sometimes I am happy to see or hear from you, but then I:
726 Sometimes I am reminded of you because:
727 Sometimes I am sensitive to:
728 Sometimes I am stressed about:
729 Sometimes I am surprised at:
730 Sometimes I am too materialistic about:
731 Sometimes I am too quick to make a judgment about:
732 Sometimes I am traumatized by:
733 Sometimes I annoy people when:
734 Sometimes I anticipate:
735 Sometimes I can picture the scene, or almost hear you say:
736 Sometimes I can't make sense of:
737 Sometimes I can't sleep because
738 Sometimes I can't stand this:
739 Sometimes I come across as having a hard heart because:
740 Sometimes I crave "this":
741 Sometimes I cry inside, but tears don't come out because:
742 Sometimes I dislike this:
743 Sometimes I do the opposite of what you want because:
744 Sometimes I do the exact opposite of what I should because:
745 Sometimes I do the exact opposite of what others want because:
746 Sometimes I do the exact opposite of what you want because:
747 Sometimes I don't bother with:
748 Sometimes I don't care because:

Conversation Starters

749 Sometimes I don't feel comfortable in the presence of:
750 Sometimes I don't feel confident that:
751 Sometimes I don't feel connected because:
752 Sometimes I don't feel heard when:
753 Sometimes I don't feel I can trust you because:
754 Sometimes I don't feel informed when:
755 Sometimes I don't feel strong because:
756 Sometimes I don't feel you are safe because:
757 Sometimes I don't get why:
758 Sometimes I don't know how to be assertive in:
759 Sometimes I don't know what to tell you because:
760 Sometimes I don't like "this" about myself or situation:
761 Sometimes I don't respond to your communication because:
762 Sometimes I don't share about "this":
763 Sometimes I don't tell others "this":
764 Sometimes I don't think "this" is reasonable:
765 Sometimes I don't think I can handle:
766 Sometimes I don't think I care about:
767 Sometimes I don't think people are comfortable around me because:
768 Sometimes I don't trust:
769 Sometimes I don't understand "this":
770 Sometimes I don't understand why:
771 Sometimes I don't want to communicate because:
772 Sometimes I don't want you to visit because:
773 Sometimes I dread:
774 Sometimes I envy:
775 Sometimes I fail to appreciate:
776 Sometimes I fantasize about:
777 Sometimes I fear "this" might be happening to you:
778 Sometimes I fear being replaced by:
779 Sometimes I fear you might think "this":

African elephants are the world's largest animals. The huge ears are shaped like Africa.

Conversation Starters

780 Sometimes I feel "it just doesn't matter as much" about:
781 Sometimes I feel "labeled" because:
782 Sometimes I feel "stuck in a rut" because:
783 Sometimes I feel, "what is wrong with me"?
784 Sometimes I feel a sense of remorse for:
785 Sometimes I feel abandoned because:
786 Sometimes I feel all alone, but I know I'm not. What encouragement could you give?
787 Sometimes I feel anger because:
788 Sometimes I feel animosity because:
789 Sometimes I feel apprehensive because:
790 Sometimes I feel awkward when:
791 Sometimes I feel betrayed because:
792 Sometimes I feel bitter about:
793 Sometimes I feel blamed because:
794 Sometimes I feel bullied because:
795 Sometimes I feel comforted by:
796 Sometimes I feel confident that:
797 Sometimes I feel conflicted because:
798 Sometimes I feel confused because:
799 Sometimes I feel depressed because:
800 Sometimes I feel desperate because:
801 Sometimes I feel determined to:
802 Sometimes I feel devastated because:
803 Sometimes I feel disappointed about:
804 Sometimes I feel disconnected from my emotions about:
805 Sometimes I feel distant from you emotionally because:
806 Sometimes I feel embarrassed because:
807 Sometimes I feel extremely bad about myself because:
808 Sometimes I feel fake because:
809 Sometimes I feel FALSE guilt because:
810 Sometimes I feel fearful because:

Conversation Starters

811 Sometimes I feel fortunate because:
812 Sometimes I feel great hope about:
813 Sometimes I feel guilty because:
814 Sometimes I feel heartbroken because:
815 Sometimes I feel helpless:
816 Sometimes I feel hostile about:
817 Sometimes I feel hurt because:
818 Sometimes I feel I abused myself when:
819 Sometimes I feel I am becoming hardened because:
820 Sometimes I feel I can't "see through the fog" because:
821 Sometimes I feel I have to be "the strong one" because:
822 Sometimes I feel I haven't been treated fairly in this:
823 Sometimes I feel I'm on a mission to:
824 Sometimes I feel I've "fallen into the cracks" because:
825 Sometimes I feel inspired by:
826 Sometimes I feel intimidated because:
827 Sometimes I feel invisible because:
828 Sometimes I feel irresponsible because:
829 Sometimes I feel isolated because:
830 Sometimes I feel it would be helpful to speak to a chaplain, counselor, or therapist because:
831 Sometimes I feel judged about:
832 Sometimes I feel judged because:
833 Sometimes I feel like a failure because:
834 Sometimes I feel like an outcast because:
835 Sometimes I feel like an outsider because:
836 Sometimes I feel like doing this positive thing:
837 Sometimes I feel like not trying that hard because:
838 Sometimes I feel like quitting because:
839 Sometimes I feel like retreating when:
840 Sometimes I feel lonely because:
841 Sometimes I feel lost because:

Ferrets emit an odor when afraid or excited and wag their tail like a dog.

Conversation Starters

842 Sometimes I feel my friends are better than my family because:
843 Sometimes I feel my resistance is low because:
844 Sometimes I feel my social skills need improvement:
845 Sometimes I feel nothing matters because:
846 Sometimes I feel overwhelmed about my responsibilities because:
847 Sometimes I feel overwhelmed because:
848 Sometimes I feel people don't care about:
849 Sometimes I feel pressure not to "open up" to you because:
850 Sometimes I feel pressure to:
851 Sometimes I feel punished for:
852 Sometimes I feel rebellious and:
853 Sometimes I feel rejected because:
854 Sometimes I feel relieved because:
855 Sometimes I feel resentment because:
856 Sometimes I feel sad because:
857 Sometimes I feel safe when:
858 Sometimes I feel shame because:
859 Sometimes I feel sorry for myself because:
860 Sometimes I feel stagnant because:
861 Sometimes I feel stuck because:
862 Sometimes I feel stupid because:
863 Sometimes I feel there is something wrong with me because:
864 Sometimes I feel too tired to get out of bed because:
865 Sometimes I feel uncomfortable because:
866 Sometimes I feel unwanted because:
867 Sometimes I feel unworthy because:
868 Sometimes I feel victimized because:
869 Sometimes I feel violated because:
870 Sometimes I feel vulnerable because:
871 Sometimes I feel weak because:

Conversation Starters

872 Sometimes I feel you act fake because:
873 Sometimes I feel you don't care about:
874 Sometimes I feel you don't love me because:
875 Sometimes I feel you have not told me "the whole story" because:
876 Sometimes I forget:
877 Sometimes I get annoyed about:
878 Sometimes I get anxious because:
879 Sometimes I get frustrated about:
880 Sometimes I get irritated about:
881 Sometimes I get jealous about:
882 Sometimes I get mad about:
883 Sometimes I get nervous because:
884 Sometimes I give one-word answers because:
885 Sometimes I have a "who cares" attitude because:
886 Sometimes I have a hard time concentrating because:
887 Sometimes I have a hard time standing by while:
888 Sometimes I have feelings of hatred toward:
889 Sometimes I have felt hopeless about:
890 Sometimes I have felt you don't care because:
891 Sometimes I have hated "this":
892 Sometimes I have nightmares about:
893 Sometimes I have so much to share with you, but don't because:
894 Sometimes I have spoken harsh words to you, but I regret it because:
895 Sometimes I hide "this" about myself:
896 Sometimes I hope:
897 Sometimes I imagine:
898 Sometimes I keep "this" in:
899 Sometimes I keep "this" secret because:
900 Sometimes I lack the courage to:

Foxes can produce over 40 different sounds and love playing with balls like a cat.

Conversation Starters

901 Sometimes I live in denial about:
902 Sometimes I make up stories about:
903 Sometimes I need reassurance that:
904 Sometimes I overcompensate in:
905 Sometimes I realize I have a problem with:
906 Sometimes I second guess myself about:
907 Sometimes I set ridiculous goals like:
908 Sometimes I shut down because:
909 Sometimes I stare out because:
910 Sometimes I struggle with admitting:
911 Sometimes I struggle with feeling I'm a loser because:
912 Sometimes I suffer because:
913 Sometimes I think, "how did I get here" because:
914 Sometimes I think "maybe today":
915 Sometimes I think "so what" because:
916 Sometimes I think, "why should I care" about this:
917 Sometimes I think about how unfair it is that:
918 Sometimes I think I'm addicted to "this":
919 Sometimes I think I'm better than "this":
920 Sometimes I think it's my fault that:
921 Sometimes I think you should already know the answer to "this":
922 Sometimes I try not to hurt your feelings, so I:
923 Sometimes I want to cry because:
924 Sometimes I want to scream because:
925 Sometimes I wish you shared more because:
926 Sometimes I wonder:
927 Sometimes I worry I might forget:
928 Sometimes I worry people will:
929 Sometimes I'm just too blunt about:
930 Sometimes I've felt like giving up on "this":
931 Sometimes it's hard to express or show my feelings because:

P.S. Please Write Back

Conversation Starters

932   Sometimes my attitude stinks because:
933   Sometimes my life is complicated because:
934   Sometimes my mind races about:
935   Sometimes others expect me to do "this":
936   Sometimes pain from the past comes crashing down on me when I think of:
937   Sometimes peer pressure gets to me and I:
938   Sometimes people get annoyed when:
939   Sometimes the expectations put on me make me feel:
940   Sometimes the weather affects me in this way:
941   Sometimes there is tension because:
942   Sometimes there's nobody to talk to because:
943   Sometimes this isn't fair:
944   Sometimes when I look in the mirror, I see:
945   Sometimes when I think of you, my heart hurts because:
946   Sometimes you don't communicate with me about:
947   Sometimes you don't take it seriously when I am upset about:
948   Sometimes you say hurtful things, for instance:
949   Sometimes your communication conflicts with other times, here is an example:
950   The "world event" that impacted me the most is:
951   The best "not" I do not regret saying is:
952   The best "yes" I've ever experienced is:
953   The best CLEAN joke I've heard this year is:
954   The best compliment I've ever received is:
955   The best fireworks show I've seen was:
956   The best homemade present I ever gave was:
957   The best impersonation I can make is of:
958   The best thing about where I am now is:
959   The best thing I cook/bake/bbq/make is:
960   The biggest adventure I've ever been on is:
961   The biggest challenge I've had this year/month/week is:

Dumpy green tree frogs have discs at the end of their toes for better grip.

Conversation Starters

962 The biggest doubt/fear I have is:
963 The biggest hassle I have to endure is:
964 The biggest obstacle I've ever had to overcome is:
965 The biggest price I've ever paid for a mistake is:
966 The biggest sacrifice I've ever witnessed was:
967 The biggest thing I've ever won is:
968 The bravest/most courageous thing I've ever done is:
969 The coldest I've ever experienced is when:
970 The craziest thing about my year/month/week has been:
971 The craziest thing that has ever happened to me is:
972 The dumbest thing I've ever said out loud was:
973 The dumbest/craziest thing my friend did was:
974 The event/situation/trial that "made me who I am today" is:
975 The fanciest place I've ever been to is:
976 The farthest I've ever walked in a day is:
977 The first time I ever got paid for working was:
978 The fragrance/smell that reminds me of you is:
979 The funniest scene I've ever watched was:
980 The funniest thing that has ever happened to me is:
981 The happiest moment of my life is when:
982 The hardest lesson I've ever learned is:
983 The hardest test I've ever taken was:
984 The hardest thing about my life is:
985 The hardest thing I've ever been forced to do is:
986 The hardest thing I've ever been through is:
987 The holiday that is hardest for me is:
988 The hottest I've ever experienced is when:
989 The kindest/nicest thing a stranger ever did for me was:
990 The last time I "acted out," it was because:
991 The last time I cried hard was because:
992 The last time I rode something powered by me was a:
993 The last time we were together:

P.S. Please Write Back

Conversation Starters

994 The last time you cried hard, what was the cause?
995 The last time you rode something powered by you was a:
996 The longest phone call I've ever shared was with:
997 The more I communicate about resentment, the more I:
998 The more we communicate, the more I feel:
999 The most amazing/impressive place I've seen is:
1000 The most annoying question I've been asked is:
1001 The most awkward situation I've ever been in is:
1002 The most costly mistake I've ever made was:
1003 The most creative person I know is:
1004 The most dangerous thing I've survived was:
1005 The most difficult decision I've ever had to make is:
1006 The most disappointing moment I've experienced is:
1007 The most emotional person in our family (and that's not a bad thing) is:
1008 The most encouraging person in my life right now is:
1009 The most enthusiastic/wildest thing I've ever done is:
1010 The most exciting event I've ever attended was:
1011 The most exciting news I've ever received was:
1012 The most exciting sport to watch, play, or hear is:
1013 The most expensive thing I've ever bought or owned is:
1014 The most expensive thing I've ever broken was:
1015 The most extravagant thing I've ever done was:
1016 The most famous person in my family tree is:
1017 The most fortunate blessing I've ever received is:
1018 The most fortunate blessing you've ever received is:
1019 The most fun I've had with friends is:
1020 The most heroic thing I've done or been a witness to is:
1021 The most hurtful, painful thing I have experienced is:
1022 The most immature thing I've ever done was:
1023 The most important issue in my life today is:
1024 The most important or memorable thing I ever lost was:

Giraffes are the world's tallest land animals. Males fight by "necking" (butting necks).

Conversation Starters

1025 The most impressive thing I can make is?
1026 The most impressive thing I know how to do is:
1027 The most interesting female in my world is:
1028 The most interesting male in my world is:
1029 The most interesting thing I've seen someone do is:
1030 The most memorable speech I've ever heard is:
1031 The most positive role model in my life at this time is:
1032 The most rewarding award/honor I've ever had is:
1033 The most rewarding thing I've done so far is:
1034 The most special/treasured memory I have is:
1035 The most supportive person in my life right now is:
1036 The most unlikely "chance encounter" I've had is:
1037 The older I get, the more I:
1038 The older you get, the more I:
1039 The reason I tell you things that no one else knows is that:
1040 The saddest experience I've ever had to endure was:
1041 The scariest ride experience I've ever had was:
1042 The scariest thing I've ever done is:
1043 The song/music that comforts/inspires me the most is:
1044 The strangest thing I've ever experienced is:
1045 The thing I avoiding share with you is:
1046 The toughest part about being apart is:
1047 The type of communication I like best with you is:
1048 The word "poverty" or "poor" brings this experience to mind:
1049 The word "soon" doesn't make sense to me anymore because:
1050 The word "worthless" makes me think of:
1051 The worst "first impression" I ever made was:
1052 The worst eating-out experience I've had is:
1053 The worst habit I've ever seen someone do is:
1054 The worst natural disaster I've experienced is:
1055 The worst part about being apart is:

P.S. Please Write Back

Conversation Starters

1056 The worst part about living where I do is:
1057 The worst purchase I ever made was for:
1058 There have been times when I worried you didn't love me because:
1059 There is a deep hole in my heart because:
1060 There's still time not to regret:
1061 These are the hopes I have for our relationship:
1062 Think of one rule you think everyone should obey and why:
1063 Think of something you believe is a terrible idea:
1064 This gives my life meaning and purpose:
1065 This happens more often than I'd like:
1066 This helps me connect to my feelings:
1067 This hurt the most:
1068 This is a "good times" memory I have:
1069 This is a "promise" I hope you do keep:
1070 This is a "promise" you haven't yet kept:
1071 This is a bad memory I have from the day you were taken away from me:
1072 This is a bad situation I didn't like seeing or being in:
1073 This is a curious thing about me:
1074 This is a fond memory I have of the last time I ate a meal with you:
1075 This is a fond memory of the last time I held your hand:
1076 This is a fond memory of the last time we laughed together:
1077 This is a fond memory of the one time we laughed together:
1078 This is a fond memory of the last hug we had:
1079 This is a good situation I loved seeing or being in:
1080 This is a personal "rule" I seldom, if ever, break:
1081 This is a quirky (weird but good) thing about me:
1082 This is a time I could never forget:
1083 This is a true story about a famous person I:
1084 This is an interesting fact about me:

Mountain gorillas laugh if tickled and cry if hurt. They eat 50 pounds of veggies a day.

Conversation Starters

1085 This is an unanswered question I have:
1086 This is how I felt when you and I became separated:
1087 This is how I hope to parent differently from this point forward:
1088 This is my favorite thing to do with you:
1089 This is my favorite thought about you:
1090 This is my happiest birthday memory of you:
1091 This is my worst "I'm lost" moment:
1092 This is one of the funniest or silliest thing I remember you doing:
1093 This is one person I feel will "be there for me":
1046 The toughest part about being apart is:
1047 The type of communication I like best with you is:
1048 The word "poverty" or "poor" brings this experience to mind:
1049 The word "soon" doesn't make sense to me anymore because:
1050 The word "worthless" makes me think of:
1051 The worst "first impression" I ever made was:
1052 The worst eating-out experience I've had is:
1053 The worst habit I've ever seen someone do is:
1054 The worst natural disaster I've experienced is:
1055 The worst part about being apart is:
1056 The worst part about living where I do is:
1057 The worst purchase I ever made was for:
1058 There have been times when I worried you didn't love me because:
1059 There is a deep hole in my heart because:
1060 There's still time not to regret:
1061 These are the hopes I have for our relationship:
1062 Think of one rule you think everyone should obey and why:
1063 Think of something you believe is a terrible idea:
1064 This gives my life meaning and purpose:

Conversation Starters

1065 This happens more often than I'd like:
1066 This helps me connect to my feelings:
1067 This hurt the most:
1068 This is a "good times" memory I have:
1069 This is a "promise" I hope you do keep:
1070 This is a "promise" you haven't yet kept:
1071 This is a bad memory I have from the day you were taken away from me:
1072 This is a bad situation I didn't like seeing or being in:
1073 This is a curious thing about me:
1074 This is a fond memory I have of the last time I ate a meal with you:
1075 This is a fond memory of the last time I held your hand:
1076 This is a fond memory of the last time we laughed together:
1077 This is a fond memory of the one time we laughed together:
1078 This is a fond memory of the last hug we had:
1079 This is a good situation I loved seeing or being in:
1080 This is a personal "rule" I seldom, if ever, break:
1081 This is a quirky (weird but good) thing about me:
1082 This is a time I could never forget:
1083 This is a true story about a famous person I:
1084 This is an interesting fact about me:
1085 This is an unanswered question I have:
1086 This is how I felt when you and I became separated:
1087 This is how I hope to parent differently from this point forward:
1088 This is my favorite thing to do with you:
1089 This is my favorite thought about you:
1090 This is my happiest birthday memory of you:
1091 This is my worst "I'm lost" moment:
1092 This is one of the funniest or silliest thing I remember you doing:

Guinea pigs get lonely, so they are happiest socializing in pairs or larger groups.

Conversation Starters

1093 This is one person I feel will "be there for me":
1094 This is one person that seems to understand me:
1095 This is one person that seems to understand what I'm going through:
1096 This is one serious issue in my life right now:
1097 This is one stupid thing I've done in my life so far:
1098 This is one way I help others:
1099 This is one way I think we could help our family keep from being for feeling distant:
1100 This is one way I use a special talent I have:
1101 This is someone you don't share enough about:
1102 This is something funny that really happened in my presence:
1103 This is something I can write about but I just can't talk with you about:
1104 This is something that makes me laugh-out-loud:
1105 This is something unusual that occurred around me:
1106 This is the best decision I've ever made:
1107 This is the best getaway/vacation/visiting memory I've ever had:
1108 This is the best way for me to let out my feelings:
1109 This is the biggest challenge I face at home/school/work:
1110 This is the farthest place I've ever been to:
1111 This is the funniest memory I have of you:
1112 This is the funniest thing that ever happened with you and I:
1113 This is the funniest thing you have ever said to me:
1114 This is the most difficult thing I have experienced:
1115 This is the most disturbing thing I've ever seen:
1116 This is the most heart-warming thing I've ever seen:
1117 This is the most traumatic thing I've been through this year/month/week:
1118 This is the only thing I don't think I could discuss with you right now:

Conversation Starters

1119 This is the most unusual pet I've ever lived with:
1120 This is the saddest thing I've ever experienced:
1121 This is the strangest thing I've ever done:
1122 This is what I am looking forward to:
1123 This is what I feel like after getting to visit with you:
1124 This is what I feel like after receiving a letter from you:
1125 This is what I feel like after receiving art/creative writing you have made for me:
1126 This is what I feel like after talking on the phone with you:
1127 This is what I have learned from my mistakes:
1128 This is what I know of my dad's childhood:
1129 This is what I know of my mom's childhood:
1130 This is what I look forward to helping you with:
1131 This is what I loved about taking care of you:
1132 This is what I remember from the day you and I were separated:
1133 This is what I think might help us bond even though we are apart:
1134 This is what I think of on New Year's Eve:
1135 This is what I want at this time:
1136 This is what keeps me going and alive:
1137 This is what you being away has done to me:
1138 This is why I feel crying in the presence of others is bad:
1139 This person has impacted my life because:
1140 This person is always there for me:
1141 This person is dear to me:
1142 This person is interesting to me:
1143 This person is often there for me:
1144 This person makes me laugh:
1145 This phone call made me the happiest this year/month/week:
1146 This phone call made me the happiest this year/month/week?
1147 This is something that really happened this year/month/week:

Hedgehogs protect themselves by tucking in body parts and curling into a ball.

Conversation Starters

1148 This song always makes me think of you:
1149 This stranger's small gesture touched me:
1150 This surprises me the most about:
1151 This usually makes me cry:
1152 This was a "turning point" in my life:
1153 Time flies when:
1154 Time slows to a stop when:
1155 To be honest, I still struggle with:
1156 To escape "feeling," I sometimes do this:
1157 Very often, I feel that sense of regret over:
1158 Waiting has taught me:
1159 We don't talk about "this", but I think we should begin discussing it:
1160 We need to get through the tough stuff that needs to be discussed. Why are you mad or upset at me (don't assume I know even if I should)?
1161 We used to be closer in our relationship, but that changed when:
1162 What "world event" impacted you the most, and why?
1163 What accomplishment are you most pleased/proud of?
1164 What advice can you give me to help me deal with:
1165 What amazing adventure would you love to take?
1166 What amazing thing have you experienced that no one was there to witness?
1167 What animal sound does your singing most resemble?
1168 What are some of the things you "can't" do because of our distance?
1169 What are some things you can do even though we are apart?
1170 What are you determined to do?
1171 What are you good at that not many people know?
1172 What are you most curious about?
1173 What are you most famous for?

Conversation Starters

1174 What are you obsessed with that others are not?
1175 What are your greatest strengths?
1176 What are your most gifted skills?
1177 What bugs you the most?
1178 What business would you start if education, experience, location, money, or opportunity were not a problem?
1179 What "cause" do you like to volunteer for?
1180 What causes you concern?
1181 What causes you to be scared?
1182 What charity, religious organization, or cause do you support and/or believe in?
1183 What cheers you up when life is hard?
1184 What could I have done better?
1185 What decisions do you need to make soon that you'd like advice on or input about?
1186 What do you enjoy watching?
1187 What do you feel would help our family unite?
1188 What do you have a strong opinion about:
1189 What do you have to practice a lot that others don't?
1190 What do you have to practice at?
1191 What do you hope happens after I am free to be with you?
1192 What do you like to collect?
1193 What do you like to do the most?
1194 What do you like to learn about?
1195 What do you like to play the most?
1196 What do you think causes you to feel out of control:
1197 What is more important for you and me: material things and money, or happiness and love with less stuff?
1198 What do you think is more rewarding, freedom, or fun (and why)?
1199 What do you want to know about me that you don't already?
1200 What gets you fired up and full of passion?

Hippopotamuses weigh as many as three small cars. They kill over 400 people a year.

Conversation Starters

1201 What gets you interested/excited/passionate to accomplish something?
1202 What gives you the most hope for our future?
1203 What gives your life meaning and purpose?
1204 What has surprised you in the last year/month/week?
1205 What have you tried to "save" me from?
1206 What I did harmed you, and I apologize for:
1207 What I do today counts, so today I will:
1208 What is a fragrance/smell that reminds you of me?
1209 What is a quirky (weird but good) thing about you?
1210 What is one "chance encounter" you feel changed your life, and how?
1211 What is one accomplishment you are proud of?
1212 What is one activity you've never tried but want to?
1213 What is one dumb thing you've learned:
1214 What is one interesting fact about you?
1215 What is one memorable "family history" story you know?
1216 What is one of the best things your parent(s) ever did for you?
1217 What is one of the stupidest things you've ever done?
1218 What is one of your favorite quotes, lines of poetry, sentences, or verses?
1219 What is one passion you have?
1220 What is one personal "rule" you seldom, if ever, break?
1221 What is one thing just by looking at you others wouldn't ever know:
1222 What is one thing you are most thankful for regarding our relationship?
1223 What is one thing you are working on that you've yet to complete?
1224 What is one thing you didn't think you would like until you tried it?
1225 What is one thing you hope you never experience:

P.S. Please Write Back

Conversation Starters

1226 What is one thing you keep meaning to do but haven't yet?
1227 What is one thing you like to do "the old fashioned way":
1228 What is one thing you like to watch people do:
1229 What is one thing you love or love to do?
1230 What is one thing you recently discovered you have been doing incorrectly (it's never too late to learn)?
1231 What is one thing you used to covet, but are now glad you never got it:
1232 What is one thing you wish you knew how to make?
1233 What is one thing you wish you were better at:
1234 What is one thing you wouldn't want your worst enemy to experience?
1235 What is one thing you'd like to be remembered for:
1236 What is one thing you've changed your belief/opinion on:
1237 What is one thing you've love to control:
1238 What is one way you have felt "let down" by me:
1239 What is something about you that surprises others?
1240 What is something odd you do with something ordinary?
1241 What is something others doubted you could do that you proved them wrong?
1242 What is something that makes you laugh-out-loud?
1243 What is something that was harder when you were younger?
1244 What is something you are amazed you won?
1245 What is something you are tired of hearing about:
1246 What is something you believe you will never experience?
1247 What is something you sometimes fail to appreciate?'
1248 What is something you think about the most?
1249 What is something you wish you still had?
1250 What is something you'd like but could never afford?
1251 What is the best CLEAN joke you've heard this year?
1252 What is the best compliment you have had this past year/month/week/day?

Hummingbirds are the world's smallest birds. They travel up to 23 miles a day at 35+ mph.

Conversation Starters

1253 What is the best compliment you've ever received?
1254 What is the best getaway/vacation/visiting memory you've ever had?
1255 What is the best impersonation you can make?
1256 What is the best thing that happened in your last year/month/week?
1257 What is the best thing that happens almost every day of your life?
1258 What is the best thing you cook/bake/bbq/make?
1259 What is the biggest adventure you've ever been on?
1260 What is the biggest doubt/fear you have?
1261 What is the biggest misunderstanding you think we have had with each other?
1262 What is the biggest sacrifice you've ever made?
1263 What is the bravest/most courageous thing you've ever done?
1264 What is the coldest experience you've ever had?
1265 What is the dumbest/craziest thing a friend has done?
1266 What is the funniest thing that has ever happened to you?
1267 What is the happiest moment of your life?
1268 What is the hardest lesson you've ever learned?
1269 What is the hardest part about calling?
1270 What is the hardest part about emailing?
1271 What is the hardest part about visiting?
1272 What is the hardest part about writing?
1273 What is the hardest thing you've ever been through?
1274 What is the hottest experience you've ever had?
1275 What is the kindest/nicest thing a stranger ever did for you?
1276 What is the most amazing/impressive place you've ever seen?
1277 What is the most annoying question you've ever been asked?
1278 What is the most difficult decision you've ever had to make?
1279 What is the most difficult disease/injury/surgery you've ever experienced?

Conversation Starters

1280 What is the most enthusiastic/wildest thing you've ever done?
1281 What is the most frustrating thing that happens almost every day of your life?
1282 What is the harshest thing I've ever communicated to you that you feel was uncalled for?
1283 What is the most heartwarming thing you've ever seen?
1284 What is the most heroic thing you've ever done, or been a witness to?
1285 What is the most immature thing you've ever done?
1286 What is the most important item you have in your room/place?
1287 What is the most impressive thing you know how to do?
1288 What is the most impressive thing you make?
1289 What is the most interesting thing you've seen someone do?
1290 What is the most likely thing to make you feel out of control of your life?
1291 What is the most memorable clothing or outfit you think you'll remember me wearing?
1292 What is the most painful experience you've had this year/month/week?
1293 What is the most painful experience you have had?
1294 What is the most painful experience you've had?
1295 What is the most special/treasured memory you have?
1296 What is the most unusual pet you've ever lived with?
1297 What is the saddest experience you've ever had to endure?
1298 What is the scariest ride experience you've ever had?
1299 What is the scariest thing you've ever done?
1300 What is the strangest thing you've ever done?
1301 What is the strangest thing you've ever experienced?
1302 What is the worst "first impression" you've ever made?
1303 What is the worst injury you've ever experienced?
1304 What is the worst purchase you've ever made?

Hyenas are vocal; they whoop, whine, and cackle. Their sounds mimic human laughter.

Conversation Starters

1305 What is your dream car (year, make, model, color)?
1306 What is your favorite activity/hobby/pastime?
1307 What is your favorite book, movie, song, theater production, or TV show?
1308 What is your favorite childhood memory:
1309 What is your favorite holiday memory?
1310 What is your favorite home-cooked meal?
1311 What is your favorite restaurant and meal there?
1312 What is your favorite sound?
1313 What is your favorite thing to do?
1314 What is your idea of a great way to have clean/wholesome fun?
1315 What is your least favorite home-cooked meal, and why?
1316 What is your life like?
1317 What is your most blessed/proudest creation/invention?
1318 What is your most irrational/unusual fear?
1319 What is your most memorable volunteer experience?
1320 What is your most-used or favorite emoji, and why?
1321 What is your sleeping place like? Can you describe your room or place so I can picture it?
1322 What is your worst "customer service" experience ever?
1323 What is your worst "seemed like a good idea" moment?
1324 What is your worst ever getaway/vacation story?
1325 What main challenge do you have in your life today?
1326 What makes you frightened?
1327 What movie/tv show could you enjoy watching over-and-over again?
1328 What musical instruments can you play?
1329 What obstacles do you need to overcome to succeed at your present goal?
1330 What one "scene of your life" do you wish you could watch?
1331 What people think about me affects me in this way:

Conversation Starters

1332 What positive things would you like to accomplish?
1333 What promises have I made that I've failed to keep?
1334 What recent situation has caused you to ponder your path?
1335 What small gesture from a stranger has touched you in the last year/month/week?
1336 What song/music comforts/inspires you the most?
1337 What substantial steps are you making to reach your present goal?
1338 What suggestions do you have that you think would help me connect with you better?
1339 What surprises you the most about me?
1340 What teacher has made the biggest positive impact on your life, and why?
1341 What type of problems do you think we might face once we can be reunited?
1342 What upcoming plans or events are you looking forward to?
1343 What would make you feel accomplished/successful?
1344 What would make you jump for joy?
1345 What would make you scream out of joy?
1346 What would you have done if you faced what I had to?
1347 What would you like to learn if lessons were free?
1348 What would you say is the event/situation/trial that "made you who you are today"?
1349 What would you say is the thing you always get/got in trouble for in school?
1350 What would you say is your greatest failure, and what did it teach you?
1351 When "this" happened, I saw more than I should have:
1352 When "this" happened, I was scared out of my wits:
1353 When "this" happened, it was so long ago, I have a hard time remembering details:
1354 When "this" happens, I think of you:

The closest "relative" to hyrax—the elephant! Rock conies (hyrax) are noted in the Bible.

Conversation Starters

1355 When "this" person cries, I feel:
1356 When "this" person died, I was affected deeply in "this" way:
1357 When "this" person is disrespectful to you, I feel:
1358 When a person shows pity toward me, I feel:
1359 When have you felt the most loved by me:
1360 When I am completely bored, this helps:
1361 When I am utterly bored, I do "this" to stay sane:
1362 When I can't stay with you, I feel:
1363 When I don't cooperate about "this," it upsets you because:
1364 When I found out "this," I was happy because:
1365 When I found out "this," It upset me because:
1366 When I get a call from you I feel:
1367 When I get an email from you I:
1368 When I get mail from you I feel:
1369 When I get pictures from you I:
1370 When I have a problem, it's tough because:
1371 When I have to leave you I feel:
1372 When I look at the moon and the stars, I think:
1373 When I made "this" mistake, I didn't consider how terribly it would affect you because:
1374 When I miss you (which is all the time), this is what I do:
1375 When I need to talk about my conflicted feelings I:
1376 When I pray for you, I often ask for this:
1377 When I revisit the past, it helps me understand how I can learn from mistakes. What mistake would you feel better about discussing?
1378 When I saw "this," it was hard:
1379 When I say: "family being together brings happiness", what does it make you think of?
1380 When I see "this" date on the calendar, I feel:
1381 When I see or hear from you, I stay focused on fighting for my freedom. It's because:

P.S. Please Write Back

Conversation Starters

1382 When I see the words "baby steps," I think of:
1383 When I see you again, "this" is what I hope:
1384 When I think of "this" about you, it makes me happy:
1385 When I think of "this" about you, it makes me sad:
1386 When I use the word "heartbroken" what does it make you think of:
1387 When I was young, I wanted to be a:
1388 When I was younger, I was scared about:
1389 when I was younger, my family say I;
1390 When I wasn't able to attend "this" event, how did it make you feel?
1391 When I'm hurting or sad, "this" helps me cope:
1392 When it comes to money, I'd rather save for what I'd like because:
1393 When it comes to money, I'd rather work for what I want because:
1394 When others cry about you, I want to also because:
1395 When you act unemotional about "this," it affects me:
1396 When you and I differ on our opinions on "this," it interferes with our relationship in this way:
1397 When you are not with me, I feel:
1398 When you did "this," it affected me because:
1399 When you do "this," I feel cared for:
1400 When you do "this," I feel loved by you:
1401 When you don't cooperate about "this," I think it harms you because:
1402 When you don't respond to me, my calls, emails, letters, or other attempts to stay in touch, I:
1403 When you kept "this" from me, it:
1404 When you made "this" decision, it affected me:
1405 When you said "this," it affected me because:
1406 When you tell me stories of your life, I feel:

Marine iguanas spend most of their time in the ocean, swimming, and eating. They sneeze.

Conversation Starters

1407 When you were an infant, I often called you this:
1408 Whenever I think of this board game, it reminds me of:
1409 Where I live, there is "this" special or unusual tradition:
1410 Where is one place you'd love to go to:
1411 Where is the farthest place you've ever been to?
1412 Which one class do you wish you had paid better attention in?
1413 Who do you go to for advice or guidance?
1414 Who is someone you find interesting, and why?
1415 Who is the most famous person in your family tree?
1416 Whom do you wish you could meet?
1417 Why did you let me be adopted?
1418 Why did you sign away your parental rights to me?
1419 Without preparation, I could give a good speech on:
1420 Writing can be a healing tool. How does writing help you?
1421 You can't handle me wanting to discuss "this":
1422 You don't know how happy it makes me when:
1423 You don't understand how happy I am because:
1424 You have a natural ability to:
1425 You have taught me patience because:
1426 You haven't share about "this" person, and I'd like to know more:
1427 You may not realize it, but you say whatever you think without a filter. It affects me this way:
1428 You say "this" often, and it makes me feel:
1429 You say things that show good intention, but what are you doing to succeed at them?
1430 You should already know "this":
1431 You should already know why:
1432 You were given your name because:
1433 You were not there for me when:
1434 You were there for me when:
1435 Your absence has made me feel:

Conversation Starters

1436 Your calls make me feel:

1437 Your emails make me feel:

1438 Your letters make me feel:

1439 Your visits make me feel:

1440 _____

1441 _____

1442 _____

1443 _____

1444 _____

1445 _____

1446 _____

1447 _____

1448 _____

1449 _____

1450 _____

Impalas can leap three times their height. Males have long lyre-shaped horns.

Wild jaguars are occasionally sighted in parts of Arizona and Texas.

Apology Wording Ideas

First, what NOT to do:
- Don't make excuses.
- Don't use the word "but."
- Don't shift the blame, deflect, redirect, or distract when giving a sincere apology.
- Don't write anything that offers a defense for your words or actions.
- Don't use the words "if," "may," "might" (own your mistakes).
- Don't be general. Be specific. Tell the person what you did that was wrong.
- Don't write "I'm sorry you feel that way" as though they are wrong *when you are!*

Statements you could personalize:
1. Again, I am truly sorry for what happened.
2. Again, please accept my apology.
3. All I can offer is my heartfelt apology for the suffering you have endured.
4. Although I can understand why you are hurt, I hope to gain back your trust.
5. Although I cannot change my mistake of the past, I have learned from it.
6. Although my heart wanted to do the right thing, I chose to do wrong.
7. Can you share what has upset you? I'm (dense, insensitive) sometimes.
8. Can you think of anything I could do to ease your pain?
9. Could you share the different ways you were offended so I could own up to it?
10. Could you write me about this, even though I imagine you are mad at me?

There are more kangaroos in Australia than Australians. Roos can leap up to 29 feet!

Apology Wording Ideas

11 Do you think you could ever forgive me for my gross error?
12 Even though I knew my (behavior, actions, words) would harm you, I did it.
13 Even though I made a mistake, I am committed to your future well-being.
14 I acknowledge my mistake when I (expound on your mistake).
15 I acted with complete disregard for you and your feelings.
16 I admit I am completely guilty. You did nothing wrong. It was all my fault.
17 I am deeply ashamed of myself. I know better. My judgment was flawed.
18 I am deeply sorry for the suffering I have caused you.
19 I am embarrassed by my (words, actions, outburst).
20 I am learning and hope I don't repeat a similar (behavior, action, incident).
21 I am learning from my mistake(s) to avoid repeating it.
22 I am not excusing my behavior when I (____).
23 I am not taking my mistake lightly.
24 I am open to alternative approaches to avoid future (situations, incidences).
25 I am sickened knowing that I caused you pain, and all you must endure now.
26 I am sincerely sorry for my bad (actions, behavior, attitude, response).
27 I am so very sorry for hurting you.
28 I am sorry for my behavior and how I treated you.
29 I am sorry for my role in what happened to you.
30 I am sorry that I let words fly from my mouth that were (mean, rude, uncalled for).
31 I am still learning how to avoid having this ever happen again.
32 I am to learning from my thoughtlessness and appreciate your patience.

Apology Wording Ideas

33. I am trying to curb my inappropriate language. Could you please forgive me?
34. I am trying to make amends for harming you.
35. I am very sorry for what I (did, said) the (other day, week).
36. I am very sorry for what I have done to you.
37. I am willing to do anything I can to help repair the damage I have caused.
38. I am willing to hear anything you communicate to me regarding my behavior.
39. I am working on learning how to be more thoughtful in my future.
40. I am working on myself to ensure (this, my bad behavior) doesn't happen again.
41. I apologize and hope to make amends with you.
42. I apologize for (inconveniencing, frustrating, harming, being rude to) you.
43. I apologize for being so inconsiderate.
44. I apologize for my misconduct.
45. I apologize for what I (did, said, accused you of).
46. I apologize to you and (my peers, co-workers, classmates).
47. I appreciate your understanding. I hope you can find it in your heart to forgive me.
48. I behaved so badly. I am ashamed of myself.
49. I am horrified by how it affected you.
50. I believe the (incident, situation, etc.) resulted from (___).
51. I believe this is a one-time error on my part.
52. I believe you are (upset, offended) by (incident, situation). Can we discuss it?
53. I can and will do better.
54. I can only hope our relationship will continue.
55. I can't even imagine the (pain, fear, embarrassment, shame) I have caused you.

Koalas aren't bears. They eat up to three pounds of eucalyptus leaves a day.

Apology Wording Ideas

56. I can't begin to express just how sorry I am.
57. I can't excuse my behavior.
58. I can't express how much I regret what I did and what it has done to you.
59. I cannot excuse myself for making such a poor decision.
60. I caused you great embarrassment, I am so sorry for making you feel that way.
61. I caused you grief, and I am so very sorry.
62. I caused you harm. You did not deserve my bad behavior.
63. I committed gross error in offending you as I did.
64. I completely failed to care for you the way I always wanted to, and still do.
65. I could have (done, said) things differently, 68 66 I am sorry for how it came across.
67. I could have handled the situation differently.
68. I could have said it a different way and still got my point across.
69. I crossed the line and hurt you when that was not my intention.
70. I deeply regret (state what you regret).
71. I deeply regret my (actions, attitude, outburst, immaturity, etc.).
72. I deeply regret my actions caused you harm.
73. I deeply regret that you ever had to (see, go through, hear) that.
74. I deeply value our relationship.
75. I did not deal with (situation) well at all!
76. I did not intend to harm you, yet in the end, that's exactly what happened.
77. I didn't set out to try to hurt you, yet that's the very thing that happened.
78. I didn't think about the fact that my "little white lie" was absolutely wrong.

P.S. Please Write Back

Apology Wording Ideas

79 I distracted (you, others) from (learning, visiting, doing your job).
80 I don't deserve your (patience, forgiveness, pardon, love).
81 I don't deserve it, yet I do hope you have within yourself to forgive me.
82 I don't have a right to deserve a second chance, yet hope you will grant that.
83 I failed both you and myself.
84 I feel just horrible for treating you in such a disrespectful manner.
85 I feel like such a jerk because I was one!
86 I genuinely regret what I (did, said, did to you).
87 I have harmed you in so many ways. Can we at least talk about this subject?
88 I have learned from (this, my, the) experience.
89 I have made a big mistake.
90 I hope for your understanding.
91 I hope my apology allows you to feel comfortable enough to write back.
92 I hope our relationship can continue.
93 I hope to earn your trust back and know it will take "baby steps" to get there.
94 I hope to have better judgment moving forward.
95 I hope to improve so that (this, misunderstandings) will not occur in the future.
96 I hope we can continue to discuss this further so your healing will continue.
97 I hope we can discuss this and mend our relationship.
98 I hope we can resolve this matter.
99 I hope you accept my apology, it was my fault.
100 I hope you and I can put this (incident, matter) behind us and move forward.

A Lemur's tail is longer than its body. The females are dominant leaders in their troops.

Apology Wording Ideas

101 I hope you can forgive me for the (damage, worry) I have caused.
102 I hope you can forgive me.
103 I hope you can forgive me.
104 I hope you can pardon me for my poor (behavior, actions, words).
105 I hope you someday understand just how sorry I am that I hurt you.
106 I hope you will be able to find it in your heart to forgive me.
107 I hope you will be able to forgive me.
108 I hope you will be able to get past my rude (behavior, comments).
109 I hurt you by my mean-spirited (behavior, action, comment, words).
110 I intend to learn and grow from this (situation, incident).
111 I intend to learn from my mistake.
112 I intent to improve.
113 I just wasn't thinking.
114 I knew all along that what I was doing was wrong.
115 I know I did not meet your expectation when I could have.
116 I know I don't deserve your grace, mercy, or forgiveness.
117 I know I have caused damage to our relationship, yet hope to repair it.
118 I know I have caused you lasting harm and consequences from my behavior.
119 I know I made a mistake.
120 I know I need to adjust my (behavior, words, gestures).
121 I know I was not (kind, loving, right).
122 I know I'm wrong, and I hope to discuss the many ways I am with you.
123 I know nobody was comfortable at my poor (behavior, interaction, tantrum).

P.S. Please Write Back

Apology Wording Ideas

124 I know you deserve better from me.
125 I know you expect (more, better) from me.
126 I know you were only trying to help me.
127 I know you feel I should know why you are offended, yet I'm clueless.
128 I know you have been severely affected by my (actions, behavior, words).
129 I know you were only trying to help me.
130 I lacked giving you the respect you deserve.
131 I lied to you when you trusted me most.
132 I look forward to (working, visiting, being) with you (again, soon).
133 I lost my temper, and it caused you harm.
134 I made a big mistake.
135 I made a commitment to you and failed to honor it.
136 I made a dumb mistake.
137 I never should have done that.
138 I owe you a big apology.
139 I really didn't intend to create an awkward situation, yet that's what happened.
140 I regret the harm my bad (action, behavior) has done to you.
141 I responded very poorly.
142 I should have been there for you, yet I failed at that.
143 I should have stopped (___) and considered how much it would harm you.
144 I should not have (done, said) what I did.
145 I should not have let my personal problems affect you.
146 I take full responsibility for my mistake. 150   147 I hope I am never as stupid again.
148 I understand I have harmed you and our relationship. I hope for reconciliation.
149 I know I need to refrain myself from (___).

A lion's roar can be heard up to 5 miles away. They run 50 mph at 36-foot leaps.

Apology Wording Ideas

150 I value (your friendship, our relationship, your insight, opinion, or perspective).
151 I value our relationship.
152 I want to (overcome, improve, succeed).
153 I want to continue to learn and grow (under your guidance, in our relationship).
154 I want to do everything I can to help you heal and fix anything possible.
155 I want you to know how deeply I regret my actions.
156 I was (wrong, stupid, dumb, an idiot, immature, not right, way off, etc.)
157 I was a complete (jerk, idiot, selfish pig).
158 I was completely wrong.
159 I was disrespectful.
160 I was disrespectful. I was wrong. You are right.
161 I was disruptive.
162 I was going through a very difficult time, though it's no excuse.
163 I was inappropriate.
164 I was selfish when I (did, said): ____.
165 I was simply not thinking when I (__).
166 I was so rude. There is no excuse.
167 Please accept my sincere apology.
168 I wasn't thinking when I make this mistake.
169 I will forever be haunted by what I did and how it affected you.
170 I wonder if you could ever forgive me.
171 Maybe not, yet I still hold onto hope.
172 I would like to express my deep regret for my (action, behavior, words).
173 I'm ashamed of what I did and how it has harmed you.
174 I'm sorry I did not value you as I should have.
175 I'm sorry I hurt you.
176 I'm sorry I hurt your feelings.

P.S. Please Write Back

Apology Wording Ideas

177 I'm sorry I made you (scared, uncomfortable, fearful).
178 I'm still learning how to handle situations differently, so I won't repeat the error.
179 I'm sorry I harmed you.
180 If I could take it back, I would, yet I own my mistake and the harm it caused.
181 If I wasn't so (stupid, out of it), I would have realized earlier the harm it caused.
182 If some good could come out of this, it is that (state what you have learned).
183 If you feel I don't get how wrong I was, would you please discuss it with me?
184 In hindsight, I should have...
185 In looking back, I want to apologize for (doing, saying, being).
186 In retrospect, I certainly would not make the same mistake as this time.
187 Is there anything else I could do to prove to you I am genuinely sorry for my actions?
188 Is there anything you know of that I could do to rectify the situation?
189 Is there something you know of that I could apologize for?
190 It is understandable that you are (angry, hurt, frustrated, offended).
191 It wasn't my intention to embarrass (you, them, everyone, family).
192 It wasn't my intention to inconvenience you, yet that is what happened.
193 My (action, behavior) was very inappropriate. I ask for your forgiveness.
194 My (actions, behavior, attitude, etc.) was not acceptable at all.
195 My (actions, behavior, words) created an unfortunate (situation, experience).

*Lynx male "toms" and female "queens" are less aggressive than bobcats.

Apology Wording Ideas

196 My (actions, words, behavior) was inexcusable.
197 My (behavior, actions) caused you so much grief.
198 My (behavior, words, actions) were extremely childish.
199 My (behavior, words, actions) were extremely disrespectful.
200 My (behavior, words, actions) were extremely disruptive.
201 My (behavior, words, actions) were unprofessional.
202 My (immoral, unlawful) behavior is inexcusable.
203 My (words, actions, comments, behavior) are regrettable.
204 My actions affected you severely. I want you to know I realize I was wrong.
205 My behavior was completely uncalled for.
206 My behavior was immature.
207 My behavior was uncalled for.
208 My behavior was very inappropriate.
209 My carelessness has caused you great harm.
210 My mistake caused you (harm, great distress).
211 Now, here are examples of wording that you can make your own:
212 Obviously, I (judged, assumed, responded) to the (incident, situation) incorrectly.
213 Please accept my deepest apology.
214 Please accept my letter as my formal apology for (___).
215 Please accept my sincerest apology.
216 Please don't blame yourself for what happened. It was entirely my error.
217 Please feel free to let me know your thoughts.
218 Please share your concerns about this (matter, incident, situation).
219 Please, would you share any thoughts you have on this?
220 Please, would you share your thoughts on my apology?
221 Pray for me to learn from my mistake.
222 Selfishly, I was only thinking of my needs,

P.S. Please Write Back

Apology Wording Ideas

      and ignored yours in the process.
223 Sometimes I am just too (blunt, offensive) and speak my mind without thinking.
224 Sadly, I did do that.
225 Sometimes I just lack wisdom and do (dumb, stupid, thoughtless) things.
226 Sometimes I make really poor decisions.
227 I'm sorry it affected you.
228 The (anger, disappointment) you have for me is (reasonable, valid, understandable).
229 There is no excuse for what I (did, said, etc.).
230 There is no excuse or justification for my sin against you.
231 There is no other way to put it. I was wrong.
232 This (situation, incident) brought out the worst in me. I was so wrong.
233 This is totally (my fault, on me).
234 To help me guard against future mistakes, could you share your insight?
235 What happened to you was unfair and I deeply regret my part in that.
236 What I feel pales in comparison to what you must be feeling and going through.
237 What I said was completely out of line. I should never have said what I did.
238 While it is no excuse, I was going through a difficult time.
239 While it is no excuse, what you didn't know is (__).
240 Words could never fully express how sorry I am.
241 Would you be (able, willing, open) to reconciliation?
242 Would you be able to grant me your forgiveness?
243 Would you be able to share a better way I could have handled (that)?
244 Would you consider being lenient in this (case, matter, incident).

Patagonian Mara (Cavy) can sit like cats, walk like deer and run up to 45 mph!

Apology Wording Ideas

245 You can't imagine how sorry I am.
246 You are a bigger person than I.
247 You are justified in being upset with me. I was so very wrong.
248 You are offended, and I am sorry (I am, my behavior is) the reason.
249 You are so valuable, and I am tortured by regret for my poor decision-making.
250 You can (count on, expect) better behavior from me from this point forward.
251 You can (count on, expect) more appropriate behavior from me in the future.
252 You can't imagine how much I kick myself for choosing wrong.
253 You can't imagine how terrible I feel that I put you in that situation.
254 You can't imagine the regret I feel.
255 You deserve much better treatment than how you were treated.
256 You deserve to be treated better than that.
257 You did not deserve any of the consequences my poor decision caused.
258 You did nothing wrong; the fault lies solely upon me.
259 You knew I was wrong before I could bring myself to admit it.
260 You trusted me. I let you down.
261 You were relying on me, and I failed you.
262 You were right to call me out on (insert specific details).

Marmots (woodchucks) hibernate up to 23 feet below ground for up to 80% of their life.

Meerkat mobs can appear as one animal to predators by standing together and hissing.

Fishing for a Response

1. Among friends or family, what are you famous for?
2. Are you usually early or late?
3. Describe a "turning point" in your life:
4. Have you ever been in a commercial, movie, the news, or on TV?
5. Have you ever saved someone's life? Describe that:
6. If someone comes to you for help, what do they usually want help with?
7. If you could ask God one question, what would it be?
8. If you could go on an amazing adventure, what would it be?
9. If you could make one rule that everyone had to follow, what rule would it be?
10. If you could only eat this "grain" (food group) the rest of your life, what would be?
11. If you could only eat this dessert the rest of your life, what would be?
12. If you could only eat this fruit the rest of your life, what would be?
13. If you could only eat this protein the rest of your life, what would be?
14. If you could only eat this vegetable the rest of your life, what would be?
15. If you could take lessons for free and have the time, what would you like to learn?
16. If you could travel back in time, what year or event would you like to observe?
17. If you had a million bucks, how would you use it to meet the needs of others?
18. If you had the money and time, what hobby would you enjoy?
19. If you had to pick one thing, what are you "famous" for?
20. If you've ever been to the "Rose Parade," what was it like?
21. Name a "teen idol" you are/were "in love" with:

Opossums eat thousands of ticks a year. They belch, growl, or play dead if threatened.

Fishing for a Response

22 Name a celebrity you are disappointed or disgusted by:
23 Name a "famous person" you are/were impressed by and why.
24 Name a CLEAN movie you wouldn't recommend:
25 Name a date on the calendar that makes you happy and why:
26 Name a date on the calendar that makes you sad and why:
27 Name a fad or trend you'd like to see return:
28 Name a fragrance or smell that reminds you of someone, or something:
29 Name a natural disaster you pray you never experience:
30 Name a surgery or injury you're glad you got through:
31 Name all the places you have gone on a missionary trip to:
32 Name an event, situation, or trial that made you who you are:
33 Name one "thing" you love and one "thing" you hate to shop for:
34 Name one fantastic thing you experienced that no one was around to see:
35 Name one or more "famous people" in your "family tree":
36 Name one personal "rule" you don't break?
37 Name one quirky thing about yourself:
38 Name one thing you "coveted," but once you obtained it felt empty or disappointed:
39 Name one thing you have a strong opinion on:
40 Name one thing you hope never changes:
41 Name one thing you really want but can't afford:
42 Name one thing you wouldn't want your worst enemy to ever experience:
43 Name someone close to you that is interesting and why.
44 Name someone who impresses you with what they've accomplished:
45 Name someone you had a "crush" on:
46 Name something in your vicinity you take for granted or fail to appreciate often:

P.S. Please Write Back

Fishing for a Response

47 Name something others are obsessed with that doesn't interest you:
48 Name something you are determined to do:
49 Name something you are good at that you don't tell others about:
50 Name something you changed your opinion/belief about:
51 Name something you like to do the old-fashioned way:
52 Name something you think everyone should do at least once in their lives:
53 Name something you will NEVER do again:
54 Name the first person you remember ever "believing in" you:
55 Name the most impressive thing you know how to do:
56 Name three things you'd like to accomplish before you die:
57 Name your dream car—year, make, model and color:
58 Share how you got one of your scars:
59 The happiest moment of my life so far is:
60 The most people I've ever lived under "one roof" with is:
61 The one thing I dislike doing but have to is:
62 Think of something you'd like to try but haven't yet:
63 This happened in college/trade/vocation school:
64 This happened in elementary school:
65 This happened in high school:
66 This happened in jr. high/middle school:
67 This is the most unusual pet I've ever lived with:
68 What "chance encounter" changed your life forever:
69 What accomplishment are you most proud of?
70 What age do you want to live to?
71 What are some small things that make your day better?
72 What are two interesting facts about you?
73 What bothers you when people do this:
74 What do you regret not doing that there's still time to do?
75 What do you want to be remembered for?

🕺 Orangutans (red-haired apes) can live to 60! Males can stretch their arms to seven feet!

Fishing for a Response

76. What do you want your epitaph (memorial phrase/statement/inscription) to be?
77. What do you wish your brain was better at?
78. What gets you fired up or full of passion?
79. What have you created that you are most proud of?
80. What is a special/fond memory from your childhood?
81. What is something you believe you will never experience?
82. What is the hardest job you've ever done?
83. What is the luckiest/most fortunate thing that ever happened to you?
84. What is the most annoying habit other people have?
85. What is the most annoying question people ask you?
86. What is the most disgusting food you've ever eaten?
87. What is the most heartwarming thing you've ever observed or experienced?
88. What is the most interesting "people watching" thing you've observed?
89. What is the most likely charity, religious organization, or cause you would give to?
90. What is the saddest experience you've ever had to endure:
91. What is the strangest thing you've ever observed or experienced?
92. What is the worst natural disaster you've ever experienced?
93. What is your favorite hobby?
94. What is your favorite thing to do?
95. What job would you be terrible at?
96. What musical instruments do you know how to play?
97. What one world event changed you, and how?
98. What or whom do you spend the most time thinking of?
99. What pets did you have or want while growing up?
100. What phone call makes you happiest?
101. What skill would you like to practice to master?

P.S. Please Write Back

Fishing for a Response

102 What situation or place causes you to feel "out of place" or awkward?
103 What small gesture from a stranger made a big impact on you?
104 What song or music comforts or inspires you the most?
105 What TV show or movie do you refuse to watch, and why?
106 What was the best compliment you've ever received?
107 What was the most memorable gift you ever received?
108 What were your favorite TV shows you no longer watch?
109 What would you say was the hardest workday you've ever experienced:
110 What's one responsibility you wish you didn't have?
111 What's the best bit of advice you have ever received?
112 What's the best thing you got from your parents?
113 What's the hardest lesson you've learned?
114 What's the most immature thing you do or have done?
115 What's your favorite genre (category/subject matter) in books or movies?
116 When was the last time you rode something that was powered by your strength:
117 Where is the farthest place you've ever been from home?
118 Who or what inspires you to be better?
119 Without preparation, what could you give a good, knowledgeable speech on?

Osprey are large wild hawks. They submerge in water to catch fish with their talons.

Otters populate from California to Alaska. Their fur is water-resistant to protect them.

Nicely Worded Statements

Below are examples of affirming, complimentary, loving, or positive statements you can borrow or personalize your correspondence.

1. An honest winner outperforms a cheater any day.
2. Could anyone have handled it better than you?
3. Even though I'm flawed, you don't reject me.
4. Even though some things are hard, you aren't.
5. Even though we all make mistakes, you learn from it.
6. Every new day brings new opportunities.
7. How did you do that?
8. I admire your ability to remain calm.
9. I always hoped you'd outshine me at (____).
10. I am curious what your opinion is.
11. I am excited to see what you will do or choose.
12. I am smiling from ear to ear.
13. I am so fortunate to have you in my life.
14. I am thankful for who you are.
15. I appreciate your insight and advice.
16. I believe in your ability to get through this.
17. I believe you.
18. I can't help but smile when I think of you.
19. I can't stop thinking about you.
20. I could never repay your kindness.
21. I feel safe sharing what I really think with you.
22. I have faith you'll make the right decision.
23. I like that you learn from your mistakes.
24. I love hearing about your dreams for your future.
25. I love how creative you are.
26. I love how kind you are to others.
27. I love it when you are happy.
28. I love it when you laugh/smile. It's contagious!
29. I love that you are gentle with others.

Nicely Worded Statements

30 I love that you are honest.
31 I love that you are open to new possibilities.
32 I love that you are so helpful.
33 I love that you are so independent.
34 I love that you are so punctual.
35 I love that you are so unique.
36 I love that you aren't afraid to be yourself.
37 I love that you don't care what others think.
38 I love that you don't feel a need to be defensive.
39 I love that you enjoy discovering new things.
40 I love that you have learned patience.
41 I love that you protect yourself from mistreatment.
42 I love that you share your opinions.
43 I love that you take your classes so seriously.
44 I love the way you challenge me to think.
45 I love you for who you are.
46 I love you just as you are.
47 I love you so much sometimes my heart aches.
48 I love your cheerful attitude.
49 I marvel at your fantastic work ethic.
50 I never tire of hearing about your life.
51 I really enjoy listening to you.
52 I really enjoy spending time with you.
53 I really enjoy writing back and forth with you.
54 I really enjoy your company.
55 I really enjoy your humor.
56 I really respect and value you.
57 I see so much good in you.
58 I tell others how amazing you are.
59 I think you are kind.
60 I think you'll make an amazing parent someday.
61 I trust you will be honest with me.

Nicely Worded Statements

62 I'm glad you are better than me at (___).
63 I'm grateful you and I can (talk, write, etc.)
64 I'm ready to listen when you have time.
65 I'm so glad you are in my life.
66 I'm so happy wonderful things happened for you.
67 I've never known you to be broken by anything.
68 It is so fun to do things with you.
69 It makes me want to bless you.
70 It takes a big person to forgive, and that is you.
71 It's obvious you enjoy learning.
72 My world is better because of you.
73 Of all the choices, you made the best of it.
74 Problems are a challenge to make you better.
75 Sometimes you have to take a risk.
76 Thanks for helping me.
77 Thanks for helping your (siblings, grandparents).
78 The "unknown" is uncomfortable, but you'll do well.
79 There is someone/thing out there to help you.
80 To me, you are awesome.
81 Trials are difficult, but they form your character.
82 We all fall short of perfection.
83 We are all imperfect.
84 What a good habit to begin!
85 What you did was so kind.
86 What you have in character money can't buy.
87 What you have in character is priceless.
88 Working hard affords much.
89 You accept compliments so graciously.
90 You act responsibly.
91 You are "a natural."
92 You are a caring person.
93 You are a forgiving person.

Parrots are demanding, live up to 55 years, and may outlive pet owners.

Nicely Worded Statements

94 You are friendly to people.
95 You are a generous person.
96 You are a good (daughter, friend, son, etc.)
97 You are a good influence on your siblings.
98 You are a good role model.
99 You are a good, fast learner.
100 You are a great team player.
101 You are a positive influence.
102 You are a super kid!
103 You are a very kind soul.
104 You are a winner.
105 You are appreciative.
106 You are beautiful inside and out.
107 You are beautiful.
108 You are brave.
109 You are courageous.
110 You are faithful and loyal.
111 You are full of so much energy.
112 You are gifted with wisdom.
113 You are good at "reaching for the stars."
114 You are good at helping others calm down.
115 You are good at inventing things.
116 You are good at not overreacting.
117 You are good at sharing happy thoughts.
118 You are good at taking charge of your life.
119 You are growing into a young man/woman so well.
120 You are growing, learning, and maturing.
121 You are honest and trustworthy.
122 You are important to me.
123 You are intelligent (you know and understand).
124 You are interesting.
125 You are kind to want to please others.

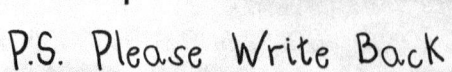

Nicely Worded Statements

126 You are loved.
127 You are loving.
128 You are making a difference!
129 You are on track towards your goal, way to go!
130 You are one optimistic soul.
131 You are persistent in pursuing good things.
132 You are persistent in what you believe in.
133 You are really good at caring for your health.
134 You are really on top of things like a pro.
135 You are reliable.
136 You are responsible.
137 You are so clever to think of that.
138 You are so deserving of sincere compliments.
139 You are so genuine you should be a gem!
140 You are so gifted.
141 You are so good to me.
142 You are so important to all of us.
143 You are so important to me.
144 You are so likable/lovable.
145 You are so mature to own your mistake.
146 You are so bright/intelligent/smart/wise.
147 You are so supportive.
148 You are so talented.
149 You are so thoughtful.
150 You are so valuable.
151 You are strong and courageous.
152 You are strong in faith.
153 You are such a bright student.
154 You are such a dependable person.
155 You are such a patient person.
156 You are such a thankful person.
157 You are the best gift I've ever received.

Emperors are the largest of penguins, 45" tall! They swim underwater over 20 minutes.

Nicely Worded Statements

158 You are the most caring/loving person I know.
159 You are the most patient person I know.
160 You are the most resilient person I know.
161 You are the only person I feel I can share with.
162 You are trustworthy.
163 You are unique; there's no one else like you!
164 You are very capable.
165 You are very compassionate.
166 You are very creative.
167 You are very thoughtful.
168 You are winning at building an excellent reputation.
169 You are wise to know when to ask for help.
170 You believe God, and that's inspiring.
171 You bring out the best in others.
172 You bring peace into my life.
173 You can "see" things others miss.
174 You can accomplish things you set your mind to.
175 You can change your mind if you want to.
176 You can do it!
177 You can learn a lot just by trying.
178 You can still choose your action and attitude.
179 You can't imagine how much I love being with you.
180 You care about doing the right thing, great job!
181 You chose right.
182 You deserve kindness, love, and trust.
183 You did well with the change.
184 You display confidence.
185 You don't have to agree with everyone.
186 You excel at overcoming difficulty.
187 You gave your best effort.
188 You get better and better every day.
189 You give so freely. It makes me proud of you.

P.S. Please Write Back

Nicely Worded Statements

190 You have a positive outlook.
191 You have accomplished so much.
192 You have a fantastic imagination.
193 You have an essential role in our family.
194 You have faced your fear with courage.
195 You have family that loves you.
196 You have friends that love you.
197 You have good insight.
198 You have many gifts and talents.  *Piglet's mom*
199 You have shown me how to have fun.
200 You have so much drive.
201 You have so much energy.
202 You have so much joy it's contagious.
203 You just keep getting better and better.
204 You learn from mistakes, unlike so many others.
205 You made a good choice.
206 You made a great decision.
207 You made a wise decision.
208 You make a difference in my life.
209 You make me believe there are some good people.
210 You make me laugh.
211 You make me smile.
212 You manage your time well.
213 You often make the best decision possible.
214 You reached your goal!
215 You really excel where others can't.
216 You see beauty in things others can't see.
217 You see what others miss.
218 You seem to absorb knowledge like a sponge.
219 You seem to be a good problem solver.
220 You seem to enjoy testing/trying new ideas.
221 You seem to have drawn inspiration from someone.

Pigs cough when annoyed, can run 11 mph, but not in a straight line, and like swimming.

Nicely Worded Statements

222 You seem to have good intuition.
223 You seem to love a challenge.
224 You seem to make friends easily.
225 You seem to understand complex problems well.
226 You should be so proud of yourself.
227 You show great respect.
228 You showed great maturity in that situation.
229 You showed wisdom when you had to say no.
230 You showed you care about others.
231 You solve problems so creatively.
232 You state the truth, and I love that about you.
233 You support the family so well.
234 You treat others with respect.
235 You were so creative in solving a problem.
236 You were so wise not to act on emotion.
237 You were there when I needed encouragement.
238 You will get through this difficult time.
239 You work so hard; you are a great example.
240 You've caused me to think differently.
241 You've given me the best compliment!
242 You've gone out of your way to help.
243 You've practiced; now you get to perform!
244 Your (mom, dad, etc.) would be so proud.
245 Your ability to forgive is remarkable.
246 Your accomplishment brought great results.
247 Your body is your own; I love that you protect it.
248 Your compassion instead of anger is impressive.
249 Your courage to "be yourself" is so inspiring.
250 Your determination sets you apart from the rest.
251 Your family loves you for who you are.
252 Your generosity is inspirational.
253 Your ideas are excellent/perfect/really good.

P.S. Please Write Back

Nicely Worded Statements

254 Your ideas matter.
255 Your kindness affected so many people.
256 Your love for family is honorable.
257 Your love helps me get through the tough stuff.
258 Your opinion matters.
259 Your personal best is all that matters.
260 Your positive thoughts are encouraging.
261 Your words are powerful.
262 Your words might not be popular, but you're right.

Polar bears are the largest meat-eaters on earth. They have black skin under white fur.

If annoyed, porcupines attack with an odor and erect quills that pierce if contact is made.

Positive Words List

Look up words in a dictionary, then create positive, encouraging statements.

Able	Addition	All	Artful
Absolutely	Adept	Alliance	Articulate
Abundance	Adjust	Allicent	Artistic
Abundant	Admirable	Ally	Ascend
Accelerate	Admire	Always	Aspire
Accept	Adopt	Amaze	Aspiring
Accepted	Adorable	Amazing	Assent
Accessible	Adored	Ambition	Assert
Acclaim	Advance	Ambitious	Assertive
Acclaimed	Advantage	Amiable	Assist
Accolade	Adventure	Amity	Associate
Accommodate	Adventurous	Amuse	Assure
Accomplish	Affable	Amusing	Astonish
Accomplishment	Affirm	Anew	Astounding
Accord	Affirmation	Angelic	Astute
Accountable	Affirmative	Animated	Athletic
Accredit	Affluent	Answer	Attain
Accrue	Ageless	Anticipate	Attempt
Ace	Agree	Anticipative	Attentive
Achieve	Agreeable	Anxious	Attest
Achievement	Aid	Appealing	Attraction
Action	Aim	Applaud	Attractive
Activate	Airy	Appreciate	Attribute
Active	Alacrity	Appreciation	Attune
Activist	Alert	Appreciative	Augment
Acumen	Alight	Approve	Auspicious
Adaptable	Alive	Aptitude	Authentic

✶ Prairie dogs bark like dogs, give nose-to-nose nuzzles, and can tunnel 100 miles!

Positive Words List

Available	Betterment	Busy	Cheerful
Avid	Bighearted	Calm	Cheers
Awake	Bizarre	Can	Cheery
Award	Bless	Capable	Cherish
Aware	Blessed	Captivate	Childish
Awash	Blessing	Captivating	Chirpy
Awesome	Bliss	Care	Choice
Aye	Bloom	Careful	Cordial
Balanced	Blossom	Caring	Chuckle
Beaming	Blunt	Casual	Chummy
Beatific	Boisterous	Cautious	Circumspect
Beatify	Bold	Celebrate	Civility
Beatitude	Bona-fide	Celebrated	Clarity
Beauteous	Bonanza	Certain	Classic
Beautiful	Bonus	Challenging	Classical
Beautify	Boost	Champ	Classy
Beauty	Bountiful	Champion	Clean
Befriend	Bounty	Change	Clear
Believe	Brave	Character	Clear-headed
Beloved	Bravo	Charisma	Clever
Benefaction	Breezy	Charismatic	Closeness
Benefactor	Bright	Charitable	Colorful
Beneficial	Brighten	Charity	Comely
Benefit	Brilliant	Charm	Comfort
Benevolence	Bubbly	Charmer	Comfortable
Benevolent	Budding	Charming	Comic
Best	Buddy	Chaste	Comical
Bestow	Build	Cheer	Commend
Better	Businesslike	Cheerful	Companionship

P.S. Please Write Back

Positive Words List

Compassionate	Contradictory	Dandy	Direct
Competitive	Contribute	Daring	Directed
Complete	Conventional	Dauntless	Discerning
Complex	Conviction	Dazzled	Disciplined
Compliment	Cool	Dazzling	Discover
Composed	Cooperate	Debonair	Discreet
Compulsive	Cooperative	Decadent	Distinguished
Comradeship	Cope	Deceitful	Donate
Conceited	Copious	Decency	Dramatic
Conciliatory	Cordial	Decent	Dreamy
Confidence	Core	Decisive	Driving
Confident	Correct	Dedicated	Dutiful
Confidential	Could	Deep	Dynamic
Confirm	Coupled	Delectable	Eager
Confused	Courage	Delicate	Earnest
Congenial	Courageous	Delicious	Ease
Congratulate	Courteous	Delight	Easily
Congratulation	Cozy	Delightful	Easy
Connected	Crafty/Artsy	Demanding	Ecstatic
Conscientious	Creative	Dependable	Edify
Conscious	Credit	Dependent	Educate
Conservative	Crisp	Desirable	Educated
Consider	Cuddly	Desperate	Effective
Considerate	Cultivate	Detail minded	Efficiency
Constant	Cultured	Detailed	Efficient
Constructive	Cure	Determination	Effortless
Contemplative	Curious	Determined	Elated
Contemptible	Cushy	Dignified	Electrifying
Content	Cute	Diligent	Elegance

⁂ Quokkas are known for their housecat size, round cheeks, and perpetual "happy" smile.

Positive Words List

Elegant	Enjoy	Esteem	Extreme
Elevate	Enlighten	Esteemed	Exult
Eloquent	Enlist	Ethical	Exultant
Embolden	Enliven	Euphony	Fabulous
Embrace	Enormous	Euphoria	Fair
Emotional	Enough	Exalt	Faith
Empathetic	Enrapture	Exceed	Faithful
Emphasis	Enrich	Exceedingly	Faithless
Emphasize	Enterprising	Excel	False
Emphatic	Entertaining	Excellence	Fame
Enable	Enthusiasm	Excellent	Familial
Enchanting	Enthusiastic	Excitable	Familiar
Encompassing	Entire	Excite	Family
Encourage	Entirely	Excited	Famous
Encouraging	Entrust	Exciting	Fanciful
Endearing	Equal	Exhilarating	Fancy
Endearment	Equality	Exhorts	Fantastic
Endeavor	Equally	Exotic	Fare
Endorse	Equilibrium	Expand	Farsighted
Endow	Equitable	Expedient	Fascinate
Enduring	Equity	Experimental	Fast
Energetic	Equivalent	Expert	Favor
Energize	Erratic	Expertise	Favorable
Energized	Erudite	Explore	Favorite
Energy	Especial	Express	Fearful
Engage	Essence	Exquisite	Feasible
Engaging	Essential	Extensive	Feat
Engross	Establish	Extraordinary	Felicity
Enhance	Established	Extravagant	Fellowship

P.S. Please Write Back

Positive Words List

Feminine	Frank	Gladness	Guidance
Fervidly	Free	Glamor	Guide
Festive	Freedom	Glamorous	Guileless
Fetching	Freethinking	Glorious	Gullible
Fiery	Freewheeling	Glory	Handsome
Fine	Fresh	Glow	Handy
Finesse	Friendly	Glowing	Happily
Firm	Friendship	Godly	Happy
First	Frugal	Good	Hardworking
Fit	Fruitful	Good-natured	Harmonious
Fitting	Fulfill	Goodness	Harmonize
Fixed	Full	Goodwill	Harmony
Flexible	Fully	Gorgeous	Hateful
Flourish	Fun	Grace	Haughty
Flourishing	Fun-loving	Graceful	Healed
Flower	Funny	Gracious	Healing
Focus	Gallant	Grand	Healthful
Focused	Galore	Grandeur	Healthy
Folksy	Game	Grateful	Heart
Fond	Generous	Gratify	Hearty
Fondly	Genial	Gratitude	Heaven
Foresee	Genius	Great	Heavenly
Foresight	Gentle	Greedy	Hello
Forgive	Genuine	Greet	Help
Forgiveness	Gift	Greeting	Helpful
Forgiving	Gifted	Grow	Helping
Formal	Give	Growing	Heroic
Forthright	Giving	Guarantee	High-spirited
Fortunate	Glad	Guest	Highly

🕺 *Raccoons have whiskers near their paws to help them "see by touch."*

Positive Words List

Hilarious	Imitative	Insightful	Justice
Hilarity	Immaculate	Inspiration	Keen
Hip	Immerse	Inspire	Kind
Holy	Immune	Inspired	Kind-hearted
Honest	Impartial	Instinctive	Kindly
Honestly	Impatient	Integrity	Kindness
Honesty	Impeccable	Intellectual	Kindred
Honeyed	Impress	Intelligence	Knack
Honor	Impressionable	Intelligent	Knowing
Honorable	Impressive	Intense	Knowledge
Honorary	Improve	Interest	Knowledgeable
Honored	Improvement	Interested	Laugh
Hope	Inclusive	Interesting	Lavish
Hopeful	Incorruptible	Intuitive	Leader
Hopefully	Increase	Inventive	Leaderly
Hospitable	Incredible	Invisible	Learn
Hug	Indeed	Invitation	Learned
Humane	Independent	Invite	Learning
Humanitarian	Individualistic	Inviting	Legendary
Humble	Industrious	Invulnerable	Leisure
Humor	Ingenious	Jewel	Leisured
Humorous	Ingenuity	Jolly	Leisurely
Ideal	Initiate	Jovial	Liberate
Idealistic	Initiative	Joy	Liberation
Ideally	Innate	Joyful	Life
Illuminate	Innocent	Joyous	Light
Illustrious	Innovate	Jubilant	Light-hearted
Imaginative	Innovative	Jubilation	Lighten
Imagine	Inoffensive	Just	Likable

P.S. Please Write Back

Positive Words List

Like	Magnitude	Metamorphosis	Novel
Liking	Maintain	Methodical	Novelty
Lively	Majestic	Meticulous	Nurture
Logical	Majesty	Miracle	Nurturing
Loquacious	Major	Miraculous	Nutritious
Lovable	Majority	Mission	Obedient
Love	Manage	Moderate	Objective
Loveliness	Manifest	Modern	Obliging
Lovely	Manly	Modest	Observant
Loving	Manner	Modify	Old-fashioned
Loyal	Mannered	Morale	Open-minded
Lucid	Marvel	Moralistic	Openhanded
Lucidity	Marvelous	Most	Openhearted
Luck	Masculine	Motivate	Openly
Lucky	Master	Motivating	Openness
Lucrative	Masterful	Moving	Opportune
Luminous	Maternal	Natural	Opportunistic
Luscious	Matter	Nature	Opportunity
Lush	Mature	Neat	Optimism
Lustrous	Meaningful	Neutral	Optimistic
Luxuriant	Mediate	Nice	Orderly
Luxuriate	Meditate	Nifty	Organized
Luxurious	Meek	Nimble	Original
Luxury	Mellow	Noble	Outgoing
Lyrical	Mend	Normal	Outstanding
Magnanimous	Merciful	Notable	Painstaking
Magnificence	Mercy	Noticeable	Palatable
Magnificent	Merit	Nourish	Paradise
Magnify	Meritorious	Nourished	Paragon

Seals can hold their breath underwater for up to two hours.

Positive Words List

Pardon	Physical	Precise	Punctual
Passion	Placid	Predatory	Pure
Passionate	Planful	Predictable	Purity
Passive	Playful	Prejudiced	Purpose
Paternal	Pleasant	Preoccupied	Purposeful
Patience	Please	Prepared	Quaint
Patient	Pleasurable	Presumptuous	Quest
Patriotic	Pleasure	Pretty	Questioning
Peace	Plenitude	Principle	Quick
Peaceable	Plenteous	Principled	Quick-witted
Peaceful	Plentiful	Private	Quiet
Peacemaker	Plenty	Prize	Quirky
Peacemaking	Plethora	Pro	Quotable
Peak	Plodding	Productive	Radiant
Pep	Plush	Proficient	Rapture
Perceptive	Poise	Profound	Rational
Perfect	Poised	Progress	Ready
Perfection	Polished	Progressive	Real
Perfectionist	Polite	Prominent	Realistic
Persevere	Popular	Promote	Reassuring
Persevering	Positive	Promotion	Receptive
Persistent	Possessive	Prosper	Reciprocate
Personable	Possible	Prosperous	Recognize
Perspective	Potential	Protect	Recommend
Persuasive	Powerful	Protected	Refined
Perverse	Practical	Protective	Refinement
Petty	Praise	Proud	Reflective
Phenomenal	Prayerful	Providential	Refresh
Phlegmatic	Precious	Prudent	Refreshing

114 P.S. Please Write Back

Positive Words List

Regard	Restful	Satisfy	Silent
Rejoice	Restorative	Saving	Silly
Rejuvenate	Restore	Savior	Simple
Relax	Restored	Scholarly	Simplicity
Relaxed	Restrained	Scrumptious	Simplify
Release	Result	Scrupulous	Sincere
Reliable	Retiring	Secure	Sincerity
Reliance	Revere	Seemly	Single-minded
Relief	Reverence	Self-control	Skeptical
Religious	Reverential	Self-denying	Skilled
Rely	Revival	Self-discipline	Skillful
Remarkable	Revolutionize	Self-esteem	Smart
Remedy	Reward	Self-help	Smashing
Renew	Rewarding	Self-reliant	Smile
Renowned	Rich	Self-sacrificing	Smooth
Repentant	Richly	Self-sufficient	Sober
Replenish	Ridiculous	Selfless	Sociable
Reputable	Right	Sensational	Social
Reserved	Robust	Sense	Soft
Resilient	Romantic	Sensible	Solemn
Resolution	Rousing	Sensitive	Solid
Resound	Rustic	Sentimental	Solitary
Resounding	Sacred	Serenity	Solution
Resourceful	Safe	Serious	Sophisticated
Respect	Safety	Servant	Soul
Respected	Sage	Sharing	Soulful
Respectful	Salubrious	Shine	Sound
Responsible	Satisfaction	Shrewd	Sparkling
Responsive	Satisfactory	Shy	Special

Barbary sheep look like wild goats with thick horns. The females are more aggressive.

Positive Words List

Spectacular	Super	Thankful	Trustworthy
Spirited	Superabundant	Thanksgiving	Trusty
Spiritual	Superior	Therapeutic	Truth
Splendid	Supple	Therapy	Truthful
Splendor	Supporter	Thorough	Try
Spontaneous	Supporting	Thoughtful	Ultimate
Sporting	Supportive	Thoughtfulness	Ultra
Stable	Supreme	Thrilled	Unaggressive
Steadfast	Sure	Thrilling	Unchanging
Steady	Surprise	Thrive	Uncomplaining
Steward	Surprising	Thriving	Unconditional
Still	Sustain	Tidy	Uncritical
Straightforward	Sweet	Timeless	Undemanding
Strict	Swell	Timely	Understanding
Strong	Swift	Tolerant	Unequaled
Studious	Sympathetic	Tough	Unequivocal
Stunning	Sympathize	Tractable	Unerring
Stupendous	Sympathy	Tranquility	Unfetter
Stylish	Systematic	Transcend	Unflagging
Suave	Tact	Transform	Unhurried
Submissive	Tasteful	Transformative	Uninhibited
Subtle	Teachable	Transforming	Unity
Succeed	Teacherly	Transparent	Unparalleled
Success	Team	Trendy	Unwavering
Successful	Temperate	Triumph	Upbeat
Suffice	Tenacious	Triumphant	Uplift
Sufficiency	Tenderhearted	True	Upright
Sufficient	Terrific	Trust	Upstanding
Sunny	Testimony	Trusting	Urbane

P.S. Please Write Back

Positive Words List

Useful	Warm	Workable
Utmost	Warmth	Worth
Valid	Wealthy	Worthwhile
Validate	Welcome	Worthy
Valuable	Welcoming	Wow
Value	Well	Xanadu
Valued	Well-bred	Yea
Vary	Well-meaning	Yeah
Venerable	Well-read	Yearn
Venerate	Well-rounded	Yes
Venturesome	Wellbeing	Yielding
Veracious	Whimsical	Zany
Versatile	Whole	Zeal
Viable	Wholehearted	Zealous
Vibrant	Wholesome	Zest
Victorious	Wholly	
Victory	Willful	
Vigorous	Willing	
Virtue	Winner	
Virtuosity	Winning	
Virtuoso	Wisdom	
Virtuous	Wise	
Vision	Wishful	
Visualize	Witty	
Vital	Won	
Vitality	Wonder	
Vivacious	Wonderful	
Vivid	Wonderment	
Vulnerable	Wondrous	

Shetland ponies are small sturdy horses under 42" tall. They are natural swimmers.

Sloths sleep up to 20 hours a day, enjoy hanging upside down, and move slooooowly!

Questions You Might Ask

1. Are you sure you have all the details?
2. Are you sure you have all the facts?
3. Can you help me understand why you said that?
4. Can you share an explanation so I can understand you better?
5. Can you share anything I have done or said that made you mad or angry?
6. Can you share anything I have done or said that you were offended by?
7. Can you share your view even though it differs from mine?
8. Can you summarize what you think now that you have more info?
9. Could you clarify what you meant?
10. Could you share the reasons why you support that?
11. Do you feel you are realistic?
12. Do you have any alternate ideas that might work?
13. Do you know of any evidence that might prove what you feel is correct?
14. Do you know what caused that to occur?
15. Do you know what happened that made you feel that way?
16. Do you think you'll ever know enough to make a decision?
17. How can you be sure you aren't just assuming?
18. How could I have worded that better?
19. I don't mean to be dense, but I don't get what I did wrong, can you share more specifically, so I get it?
20. If you did choose to do that, what might be the outcome or possible consequences?

Squirrels can leap ten times their length. Their hind legs are double-jointed.

Questions You Might Ask

21 If you were to ask me the same question, how would you have worded it better?

22 In what way does your opinion differ from what I said?

23 In what ways could you have improved your chances for a better outcome?

24 Is it possible you are stuck on negative thoughts?

25 Is there anything you feel I need to apologize for?

26 What could I do to make it up to you?

27 What did you contribute that helped others get through tough times?

28 What do you think you did well?

29 What makes you curious about the situation?

30 What mistake would it have been better that you never made?

31 What question do you think might be helpful to ask?

32 What question would you ask?

33 What things have you tried that worked in the past?

34 When you used the word ___, how would you define it?

35 When you said the word ___, what did you mean by it?

Tigers are larger than lions. Unlike house cats, tigers like to swim. They can run 40 mph.

Things Kids Might Want to Know

1. Did I do something wrong? Is that why you aren't home?
2. Do you still love me?
3. Have you ever struggled with making bad decisions?
4. How long are you going to be gone?
5. Is there anything I can do so you'll get to come home?
6. Sometimes I get mad, sad, or angry because I miss you, is that normal?
7. What did you do that caused you to be taken away from me?
8. What do you do all day where you are?
9. What happens after a person dies?
10. What mistakes do you regret?
11. When are you coming home?
12. When can I come to see you?
13. Where are you at?
14. Who is going to take care of me while you are gone?
15. Why are you away from me right now?
16. Why can't I call or text you when I want to talk with you?
17. Why do bad things happen?
18. Why do people get sick or die?
19. Why do some people do bad things?
20. Why don't you and daddy get along?

1. Here are things I am worried about:
   ❏ before ❏ during ❏ after visiting:
2. Here are things that might be hard:
   ❏ before ❏ during ❏ after visiting:
3. Here are thoughts about how I feel:
   ❏ before ❏ during ❏ after visiting:
4. Visiting with you ❏ would be ❏ will be ❏ was:

Weasel young are called "kittens." Groups are called a boggle, gang, pack, or confusion.

Statements/Questions to Talk with Teens

1. Are you "on track" to finishing high school or your G.E.D.?
2. Do you believe in God Almighty?
3. Do you consider yourself a Democrat, Republican, or ???
4. What are your plans for moving out to be on your own one day?
5. Have you applied to enroll in college, trade, or vocational school?
6. If you could move, where would you like to live, and why?
7. If you had more money, what would you do with it?
8. In what way would you like me to assist you more.
9. Is military service something you would be interested in?
10. Name one thing adults "don't get" about kids.
11. Name one thing you don't know about me but wish you did.
12. Name one thing you think I should have stopped you from doing.
13. Name one thing you'd like to learn.
14. Name something fun we could do together.
15. Name the best gift you've ever received.
16. Name your top three favorite movies.
17. What do you believe happens after a person dies?
18. What famous movie quote or line do you like to repeat?
19. What in life seems unfair?
20. What is the hardest thing you've ever had to do?
21. What is the most embarrassing thing I've ever done?
22. What is the saddest thing you've ever experienced?
23. What is the worse thing a bully has ever done?
24. What is the worst thing about your situation at this time?
25. What is your favorite holiday and why?
26. What makes you feel unsafe at times?
27. What would be your "dream" family vacation?
28. What would be your dream job?
29. Who is your favorite teacher, and why?
30. Who or what scares you or makes you feel uncomfortable?

Wombat poo is shaped like a cube. Their pouches face backwards to protect their joeys.

Loving Letter Endings

1. Another way to respond to love? *Ditto*
2. God blessed me with you.
3. I adore you.
4. I always want you by my side.
5. I am so fortunate to have you.
6. I am so thankful for your love.
7. I am thankful for you.
8. I appreciate you.
9. I can't wait to see you again.
10. I care about you *a lot!*
11. I care for you with all my heart.
12. I cherish our love.
13. I could have done better, I'll improve.
14. I don't know anyone as loving as you.
15. I doubt anyone loves you as much as I.
16. I love to listen to you.
17. I love you from the bottom of my heart.
18. I love you.
19. I love your letters.
20. I miss you terribly.
21. I miss you so much, sending my love.
22. I need you in my life.
23. I never knew joy till you came along.
24. I respect you.
25. I treasure our relationship.
26. I value you.
27. I want you to be happy.
28. I wish I was there with you right now.
29. I'm a better person because of you.
30. I'm committed to trying to do better.
31. I'm happy when you are.
32. I'm motivated because of your love.
33. I'm not the same when we are apart.
34. If I were perfect, I'd have done better.
35. Thank you for forgiving me.
36. We'll be together for all eternity.
37. What could be better than loving you?
38. You are a gift from God.

*Zebra stripes are unique to each and can serve to confuse predators.

Loving Letter Endings

39 What I wouldn't do for you. With all my love.
40 You are always there for me.
41 You are more important.
42 You are my love.
43 You are my one and only.
44 You are my sunshine.
45 You are precious to me.
46 You are so special to me.
47 You are the love of my life.
48 You bring more joy than a new puppy.
49 You can't imagine how much I love you.
50 You fill my heart with gladness.
51 You help me stay strong.
52 You light up my day.
53 You make me forget difficult things.
54 You make my world a better place.
55 You matter to me and many others.
56 You mean so much to me.
57 You mean the world to me.
58 You're my sweetie, sunshine, beloved.
59 You're perfect in my eyes.
60 You're the best.
61 Your love is amazing.
62 Your love and smile is contagious.
63 Your support is so kind and loving.

Abbreviations & Acronyms

The newer way of communicating through text/chat is minimizing keystrokes on a computer keyboard or electronic device. Your child might enjoy that you "speak" their language. Write using the fewest letters possible in a word yet in a way others can still understand. Here's a start:

?4U	I have a question for you
<3	Sideways heart (love you)
2MORO	Tomorrow
ATM	At The Moment
B/C	Because
B4N	Bye For Now
BCNU	Be Seeing You
BFF	Best Friends Forever
BRB	Be Right Back
BTW	By The Way
DBE	Don't Believe Everything
DWBH	Don't Worry Be Happy
FWIW	For What It's Worth
FYI	For Your Information
GR8	Great
HAK	Hugs And Kisses
HAND	Have A Nice Day
IDK	I Don't Know
IKR	I know, right.
ILY or **ILU**	I Love You
IMO	In My Opinion
IRL	In Real Life
ISO	In Search Of
J/K	Just Kidding
JIC	Just In Case
K	Okay
LMK	Let Me Know
LOL	Laughing Out Loud
NAGI	Not A Good Idea
NM	Never Mind
NP	No Problem (or Nosey Parents)
NTS	Note To Self
NUB	New person (newbie)
NVM	Never mind
OFC	Of course
OIC	Oh, I See
OMG	Oh My Goodness
OT	Off Topic
PLS or **PLZ**	Please
POV	Point Of View
RAK	Random Act of Kindness
RBTL	Read Between The Lines
ROTFL	Rolling On The Floor Laughing
RT	Real Time
RTM	Read The Manual
SITD	Still In The Dark
SMH	Shaking My Head
SOL	Sooner Or Later
SRSLY	Seriously
SWAK	Sealed (or Sent) With A Kiss
TBH	To Be Honest
THX or **TX** or **THKS**	Thanks
TIA	Thanks In Advance
TLC	Tender Loving Care
TMI	Too Much Information
TTYL	Talk (type, text) To You Later
TYVM	Thank You Very Much
VBG	Very Big Grin
VSF	Very Sad Face
WU	What's Up?
WYWH	Wish You Were Here
XOXO	Hugs and Kisses
YOLO	You Only Live Once
YW	You're Welcome

Red pandas stand on hind legs if threatened and look like little Ewoks the size of a cat.

Ideas to Make Mail Interesting: (˙ ˙)

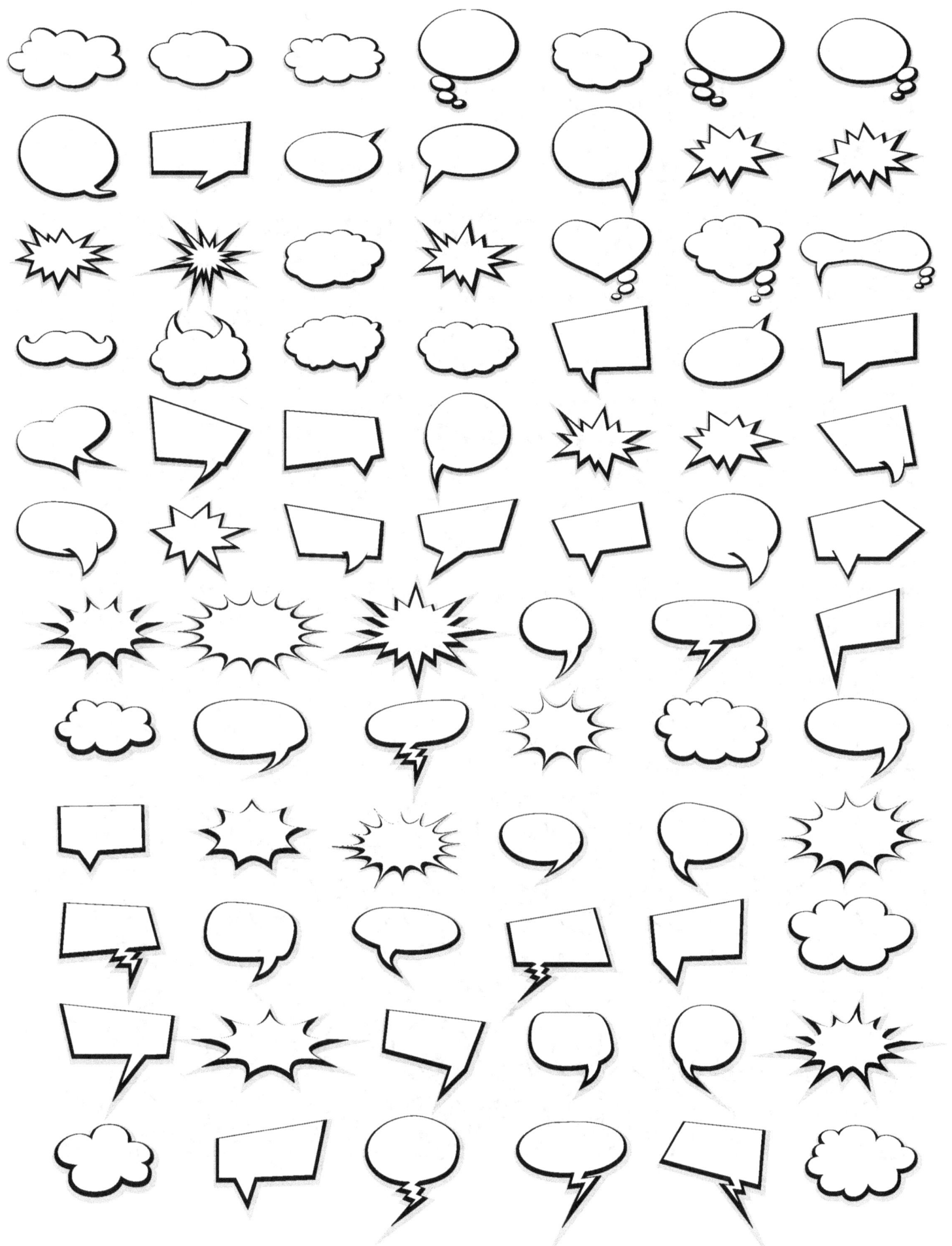

P.S. Please Write Back

Emoticons & Doodle Art

135

(Place a blank sheet over this guide to write without lined paper)

P.S. Please Write Back

www.ingramcontent.com/pod-product-compliance
Lightning Source LLC
Chambersburg PA
CBHW080225100526
44583CB00020BA/2616